DATE DUE

JUN 1 3 1994			

HIGHSMITH 45-220

GRADES AND GRADING
PRACTICES

GRADES AND GRADING PRACTICES

Obstacles to Improving Education and to Helping At-Risk Students

By

CHARLES H. HARGIS

Department of Special Services Education
The University of Tennessee
Knoxville, Tennessee

CHARLES C THOMAS • PUBLISHER
Springfield • Illinois • U.S.A.

Published and Distributed Throughout the World by

CHARLES C THOMAS • PUBLISHER
2600 South First Street
Springfield, Illinois 62794-9265

© *1990 by* CHARLES C THOMAS • PUBLISHER

ISBN 0-398-05660-9

Library of Congress Catalog Card Number: 89-29538

With **THOMAS BOOKS** *careful attention is given to all details of manufacturing
and design. It is the Publisher's desire to present books that are satisfactory as to their
physical qualities and artistic possibilities and appropriate for their particular use.*
THOMAS BOOKS *will be true to those laws of quality that assure a good name
and good will.*

Printed in the United States of America
SC-R-3

Library of Congress Cataloging-in-Publication Data

Hargis, Charles H.
    Grades and grading practices : obstacles to improving education
and to helping at-risk students / by Charles H. Hargis.
        p.   cm.
    Last in a trilogy; the 1st, Curriculum based assessment; the 2nd,
Teaching low achieving and disadvantaged students.
    Includes bibliographical references.
    ISBN 0-398-05660-9
    1. Grading and marking (Students) — United States.
2. Underachievers — United States.   I. Title.
LB3051.H343   1990
371.2'721 — dc20   89-29538
                                                                        CIP

PREFACE

This little book is the third in a trilogy directed to educational reform. The first was *Curriculum Based Assessment: A Primer*, the second *Teaching Low Achieving and Disadvantaged Students*. Each of these books directs some attention to the obstacles that grading practices create to improving the quality of American education and to helping students who are at risk. This work is a fuller exploration of the problems caused by grades.

My thanks go to Linda Hargis for her helpful review and comment.

C. H. H.

CONTENTS

GRADES AND GRADING
PRACTICES

Chapter 1

OVERVIEW

My interest in grades and grading practices emerged gradually. The conceptions I developed were influenced by my perspective in special education. These conceptions were further influenced by working with an evaluation system called curriculum-based assessment. I had been engaged at length with the problems associated with the identification and classification of exceptional children when it became clear that grades were a constant factor.

The fundamental fact in the identification of exceptional children is that they are identified by failing grades. Our primary identification tool is our grading system. Most children who are referred to determine eligibility for special education services have been so because of failing grades.

This is such an obvious notion to most that the immediate reaction to the above statement is, "So what!" We have come to assume that failing grades are a symptom of learning handicaps and disabilities. Nagging questions kept recurring to me, nevertheless. Are grades simply evidence, merely symptoms, of learning handicaps and disabilities? Could there be an error in this logic? Have we made erroneous assumptions about grades? Are they really just objective evidence of learning handicaps?

I have come to the conclusion that our reasoning has been faulty. I believe that grades are not merely symptoms but primary causes of many learning problems. This book will review the problems caused by grades and then pose alternatives to the evaluation systems that require destructive grading practices.

We have a powerful need to grade. Things with the same position, standing, characteristics, or value are grouped together. Oranges, apples, and eggs are graded according to size, color and quality and they, like children, are given letter grades.

Grades are an institutional part of American education. Grades are used to divide the curriculum, and a grade is a stage in the curriculum.

It is also a year's work. The typical curriculum is ordered in a sequence of thirteen grades.

The dominating attribute used for grading students is chronological age. Students who have birthdates within certain boundaries are placed in the same grade. Once in their assigned grade, their performance relative to other students is further graded. They may be assigned to one of several reading groups, depending on their performance in reading. Their relative performance in the group is also graded. The most usual procedure for grading performance is with letter grades.

In spite of our best efforts at grouping and grading students into increasingly homogenous units, variation within each grade or group will persist. Direct evidence of this is provided by the distribution of letter grades that is produced by the students within each of the grades or groupings.

For example, if we check the scores on the weekly spelling test in any elementary classroom, it would surprise no one to see a wide range of scores and resulting grades. The same range would be found if we checked other tests or assignments that are routinely given. The fortunate students get the A's; the unfortunate ones get the D's and F's.

We expect our grouping and grading practices to solve all problems with variability of academic aptitude. However, the distribution of grades which is produced when an instructional task is given to a group of students always confirms the continued existence of variability.

Occasionally, we find ourselves in two contradictory positions simultaneously. We want all students to do well while at the same time we want to have rigor in our grading system. We must maintain standards; we have to be tough. These opposing positions produce a dilemma not easily resolved when we blindly accept the institution of grading.

The underlying reason for the distribution of grades is that one level of instruction is given. The variability in grades is simply indicative of the variability, the individual differences, in learning ability and readiness of the students who undergo the instruction.

Academic ability exists on a continuum. It does not lend itself too well to grouping and tracking practices. Grouping and tracking are used to narrow the range of differences so that one level of instruction can be directed to each group. But there remain students at the high and low ends of the ability range, and they are out of tolerance with the level of instruction offered. Better to find the level of instruction too easy than too difficult, but either position is not the optimal one for either the high or low achievers in any group.

Students in the extremes often share more learning and aptitude characteristics with students in groups or grades below or above them. Even if action is taken to move the student through either retention or acceleration, the movement is usually done at the end or beginning of the year, the year being the grade's time unit. Consequently, acceleration or retention is done in the curricular lock step.

Perhaps a concrete illustration using chronological age is in order. Children begin the first grade of the lock-step curriculum if their sixth birthdate falls before some arbitrarily selected date at the beginning of the school year. They then are supposed to move through the grades with students who became age six between the twelve-month period prior to this cutoff date. Even though this supposedly keeps the students with their age-mates, the younger students in each grade will be closer in age to the older students in the grade below than they are to most of the students in their own grade. Conversely, the older students in any grade will be closer to the younger students in the grade above.

The same condition exists for academic ability as for chronological age. The low-achieving students are closer in ability to the students in the grade below, and the high-achieving students are closer to students in grades above. The differences in academic ability are much greater than differences in chronological age. The range of academic ability, excluding all handicaps, in almost any first grade classroom is at least 2.5 years. Chronological age range is only twelve months, but the range of academic ability in the same students is over thirty months! The range in chronological age will stay the same as a group of students moves up the curricular ladder. However, the range in academic ability actually increases and will more than double by the time the students are in high school. These facts can be verified by examining the normative data for any popular standardized achievement test.

Consider the normative data from the *Peabody Individual Achievement Test* (1970). At the first grade level, the raw scores range from 40 to 180. The grade equivalents for these scores are 0.2 to 3.9. This is a range of 3.7 years! If the range is further reduced to include the fifth percentile through the ninety-fifth, the grade equivalent range is 0.5 to 3.4. The range is still 2.9 years! This is the kind of range in achievement and ability that first grade teachers can anticipate every year.

When I demonstrated what the range was when the top and bottom 5 percent was removed, I was eliminating the majority of the students who could ultimately be classed as exceptional (Stone, Cundick, & Swanson, 1988), either handicapped or academically gifted.

Consider the range in achievement that exists in subsequent grades through the fourth grade; again the fifth through the ninety-fifth percentiles are shown: At the second grade the range is from 1.1 to 5.3, or 4.2 years. At the third grade the range is 1.9 to 7.1, or 5.2 years. At the fourth grade, the range is 2.5 to 8.7, or 6.2 years. It is quite evident that the normal range of achievement is remarkably wide, and it continues to widen the longer the students stay in school.

Grouping by grades and tracking are efficient means of dealing with a majority of students but ineffective as methods of dealing with extremes in individual academic differences. Why do we impose this practice on all students? It is administratively easier. A majority of the students are able to achieve adequately in the system, so we have deluded ourselves into believing it is appropriate for all students. The grade is the standard of performance and the level by which achievement is gauged.

Performance relative to grade placement is indicated by letter grades based on percentage scores or by letter grades based on a curve. Sixty years ago, the grading systems based on curves were introduced (Cureton, 1971). The most common is the 6-22-44-22-6 curve. The six at either end corresponds to the number of F's and A's. The twenty-two's are the number of D's and B's, and the forty-four represents the number of C's.

Most teachers don't adhere to this distribution when assigning grades. After all, as Glasser (1971) pointed out, each semester three or four students will fail in virtually every classroom of about thirty students. This means that about 12 percent fail. Percentage grading systems are apparently much more severe than grading systems based on curves.

Letter-grade distributions are simply a reflection of the difference in academic skill and achievement that exist in every classroom, given one level of instruction. We should know beforehand that if we give instructional tasks with one level of difficulty to a group of students whose ability varies over many levels, we will get a distribution of grades. If we already know this beforehand, why do we even bother giving grades?

One reason we give grades may be that we feel the need to classify (grade) children. We want to know which of the children are the most and least able. Grades are, in a sense, the primary diagnostic tool. Children who continually get poor grades are identified for further assessment to see if they can be classified as learning disabled. The first step in the diagnostic process is virtually always failing grades.

One fact that should be noted from the use of grades is the distribution of grades is directly tied to the range of levels of instruction being provided. One level of instruction at grade level will produce a wide distribution of grades resembling a normal curve. This will be true if the students in the class are typical. This distribution of grades is primary evidence that individual differences among the students in the class are being ignored. The teacher is strictly adhering to grade-level instruction.

A teacher might attempt to provide instruction at a level that was within the threshold of ability of all of the students in his or her classroom. This would still be one level of instruction, but it would be easy enough for even the slowest students to manage. The distribution of scores and grades now would be heavily skewed toward the "A" end. This would be fine for the slow students, but it would be disastrous for the more able ones.

A teacher might attempt to provide a level of instruction to be appropriately challenging for the more able students in the room. The distribution of scores and grades now will be skewed toward the "F" end of the curve. This would be fine for the most able students but disastrous for the rest. The use of a single level of instruction always has negative effects for some students.

The grading system itself perpetuates the use of single-level instruction. We think we must give grades, and we think we must give a complete distribution of grades. We can't give all students high grades. That is what grade inflation is. The simplest way, then, to make sure that we get the necessary distribution of grades is to give a single level of instruction which will induce the necessary variation in performance to which we can easily assign grades.

Having a grading system legitimizes giving failing grades. We have a grading system that includes F's and D's. We must maintain standards. We must avoid grade inflation. As a consequence of all these reasons, we must give the failing grades. The only way we can give enough students failing grades is by giving them work that they will fail at doing. The simplest way to do this is to provide only grade-level instruction. The grades, themselves, thereby legitimize both failing grades and single-level instruction.

Since we assume that everyone should only work at one level, all our attempts at individualizing instruction, remediation, or motivation are directed at trying to make students work up to grade level. Our notion of individualizing instruction is perverted by the system. Many think that individualized instruction is simply individual attention, one-to-one tutoring, or working with small groups. We do not consider the fact that individualization of instruction must, for the most part, be directed at providing instructional activities of appropriate difficulty to students. Classrooms using truly individualized instruction will have multilevels of instruction. Levels of difficulty will match every student's academic ability.

In classrooms where there is truly individualized instruction, no distribution of grades can result. The only way progress can be gauged is through direct observation of what specific skills the student is working on, the amount of progress or achievement on these skills over time, or comparison to grade peers of skills attained on the curricular sequence. Individualized instruction produces acceptable, not poor or failing performance in each student. Levels of instruction are provided for each student that are doable, not frustratingly difficult. Instructional-level activities by definition produce scores that are indicative of comprehension and learning. The high performance necessary for this cannot possibly be assigned a failing grade.

Possibly the most destructive consequence of using grades is that poor performance is blamed on the student. If a student is failing, it is that the student has a problem which is preventing him from achieving to grade level. It is expected that some students will fail. It is not the fault of the curriculum that low-achieving students fail; it is their fault. The fact that we have grading curves and letter grades leads us to believe that it is appropriate and even desirable for some students to be failing.

Having grades perverts the use of assessment. Tests are a routine part of school activities. The problem is they are used primarily to give grades. Informal tests are given periodically. Also, any instructional activity that is scored or graded is a form of assessment. When teachers evaluate the work the students do, it is primarily for the purpose of determining a grade. Only secondarily does the evaluation suggest a change in instructional activity. The results of this scoring is noted in a grade book and the cumulative results produce a final grade.

Assessment should be used primarily for evaluating the quality of the match between the student and the instructional activity being used. Poor scores or grades mean a poor match is made and an adjustment in the instructional procedure or materials is in order. Assessment should be used to assess strengths and weaknesses in the instructional process, not in the student. Grades cause us to shift the focus completely.

Most assessment only provides a passive reflection of how students perform on a level of instruction. Assessment should be an active component of instruction to be used to monitor the match between student and instruction. Assessment should be used to provide the level of instruction for each student that produces achievement and success. However, since we are bound by the need to assign grades, assessment has become a passive, instructionally useless, activity.

Grades not achievement have become the objective. This may not have been intentional, but it is the net effect of using grades. We push students to work harder to improve performance on grade-level work in order to get better grades. We should be pushing the curriculum around to fit the students to permit them to work fruitfully at their own instructional level.

Despite awareness of the negative features of grades that have been cited so far, there are individuals who still hold the view that grades have an important function. They should be used to motivate students. Poor grades should be used to make students do better. I will grant that a poor grade can nudge some students to better performance. However, this can only be done if the student is in fact capable of a higher level of performance. In other words, there is a negative discrepancy between the grade he is receiving and the grade normally assigned to students in his portion of the ability distribution. He is already capable of getting better grades, so a poor grade may cause him to improve his performance.

Such a practice will, however, not be motivating for low-achieving students. Certainly not if there is a discrepancy between his ability and the work he is being required to do. Poor grades will not motivate these students; poor grades will demoralize them. Chronic failure produces and magnifies a variety of behavioral difficulties that have a very negative effect on a student's motivation.

The grades that are motivating are good grades (Evans, 1976). Consequently, the only students who are motivated by grades are students who are already getting good grades.

Chronic failure is not productive. As Glasser (1971) pointed out, "all you learn from failing is how to fail." A student cannot learn adequately unless he is performing well. We accept and expect a range of grades, so we accept and expect a range of performance levels. We should not be accepting of this. High levels of performance need to be made possible for all students.

Good performance means more than simply getting good grades. It means that the daily work being done by the students is being done correctly and successfully. More simply put, you must get the right answers in order to learn the right answers. Much more will be said about the issue of success and failure in subsequent chapters. For now, it should be noted that success is fundamental to achievement. Lack of success means lack of achievement. Failing grades are indicative of our failure to provide success for most students who receive them.

Low-achieving and disadvantaged students should not be penalized simply because they are low achievers. They deserve work that they can do successfully. They deserve it not only for humane reasons but because success is necessary for adequate achievement. Lack of success produces the myriad of problems the low-achieving and disadvantaged students have.

The requirement that all students must be successful is contradictory to a grading system. If all students must be successful, then it will be demonstrated in the work they do. They will be showing the same performance or scores on the work they are doing as their high-achieving peers. Granted, the work will be at different levels of difficulty, but the indexes of performance, the scores, will be the same. Since the scores must be uniformly high, it will be virtually impossible to have a grading system of the type we do now.

Grades are not passive indexes of student performance. They are, for example, not just a symptom of low achievement. The existence of grades is a definite, active contributory factor in the educational difficulties of low-achieving, learning disabled, and disadvantaged students. Grades are a primary factor in students' dropping out of school.

Chapter 2

HISTORY OF GRADES

Grades are such an ingrained part of our educational system we assume that they have always been with us. This, however, is not the case. Grades are a relatively new phenomenon. There is not much evidence of their use prior to the mid-nineteenth century.

It was not until the mid-nineteenth century in Europe and the United States that public education became widespread and that marking and grading systems came into use (Kirschenbaum, Napier, & Simon, 1971; NEA, 1974). Prior to this time there is no indication of any real purpose for grading. In learning a skilled trade, an apprentice was judged competent by his master and was then permitted to join the guild and become a journeyman. A student wishing to enter a university would be examined, but again there were no grades given; either the prospective student passed or he didn't.

Wealthy students had tutors and private schools. For the less wealthy, there were subscription schools. For the poor, there was nothing except what was passed from parent to child. Examinations when they were given were not for the purpose of giving grades. They were used to show student progress, and they were used to see what additional work a student might need in order to get into college and handle the work there.

Up until about 1850 most schools were of the rural, one-room variety. Students of all ages were mixed together and most students did not stay in school beyond the most elementary levels. The curriculum content was simple. The focus was on reading, writing, and arithmetic. Some work on history and geography might have been provided. The students generally demonstrated their competencies by reciting. Progress was indicated descriptively; the teacher would simply write down the skills a student had or had not acquired. This was done primarily to indicate when a student was ready to move on to the next level or subject area.

Before 1850 most elementary schools in the United States were the one-room kind, and most students still did not attend school beyond

11

elementary levels. After 1850, the number of government-supported elementary schools increased. From 1850 to 1870 the number of students attending school increased from 13 percent to 20 percent. As the number of students increased, the students were organized according to age and the schools gradually became graded. The passage of compulsory attendance laws at the elementary levels caused a great increase in the number of students attending school. Consequently, the number of students attending secondary schools also increased. From 1870 to 1910 the number of public high schools increased from 500 to 10,000 (Kirschenbaum et al., 1971).

The elementary schools still used written descriptions to describe student progress, but the high schools began to use percentage scales or scales of 1 to 100. This was the beginning of the grading system we know today. One of the reasons for developing this grading system was to help teachers differentiate among students of various academic abilities. It helped in fitting students into the grades and tracks that were increasingly used as schools became larger and more grade levels and subject areas were included in the curriculum. One form of grading, the age- and ability-level grades, fostered and encouraged the development of the other form of grading. A student now could be compared to others in his class or age group. They then could be further segragated in more homogeneous ability groups with the intent of making mass education more efficient.

In addition to the classifying function of the emerging grading systems, grades had another important function. Competition for admission to colleges had become a problem with the great expansion in enrollments at public high schools. Scores or grades were used to help colleges screen applicants. These grading systems, it should be noted, had no educational function other than to classify, group, or qualify students.

Colleges and universities had already been using a variety of classification systems (Cureton, 1971; Milton, Pollio, & Eison, 1986). Yale was the first university in America to use a grading system. It had four classifications for students: Optime, Second Optime, Inferiors, and Perjores. In 1891, the University of Georgia was using a three-point grading system. One was the highest mark, two was medium, and three indicated deficiency. An asterisk with the one meant outstanding excellence.

Cureton (1971) described a problem that emerged with grades and continues to the present: grade inflation. She described this problem of a Virginia academy who had classified its students into six categories:

optimus, melior, bonus, malus, perjor, and pessimus. The president of the institution had complained of the continual tendency to mark the poorer students too high. He claimed that not half the bad students got malus, and the worst students seldom were below it. Also, bonus which should have been considered a high mark was instead considered a disgrace by many students, and optimus, which should have been given only to students of the highest merit, was commonly given to any student who rose above mediocrity. The president attempted to rectify this problem by instituting a new grading system with only three categories, distinguished, approved, and disapproved. However, he then complained that within two or three years some bad scholars were approved and almost all the good students were classified as distinguished.

By the turn of the century, especially in the secondary schools, percentage grading became increasingly popular. However, many elementary and some secondary schools were still getting along without any grading, or with just a few symbols, such as an S for satisfactory or a U for unsatisfactory (Kirschenbaum et al., 1971).

During the private and subscription school era, a student's progress was attributable to the teacher. In effect, the teacher was graded based on the performance of her or his students. However, under grading systems, the responsibility for achievement was shifted to the student. Grading was becoming the responsibility of the teacher and learning the responsibility of the student. Under the older system if the students didn't make satisfactory progress the teacher's job was in jeopardy. Now, in graded systems, achievement, rather than being indicated as a list of individual attainments, became only an index by which an individual could be compared to the standard of grade placement and curriculum.

Grading systems became gradually more widespread. Eventually, however, the indexes themselves came under critical scrutiny. The reliability of 100-point scales and percentage grading systems came into question. In 1912 Starch and Elliot (1912) published the results of a study which sharply criticized the reliability and objectivity of teachers' judgment in using these grading systems. These two researchers wanted to determine the extent of subjectivity and imprecision in teacher judgment using a 100-point scale. To do this they obtained copies of two English papers written by two students at the end of their first year in a large Midwest high school. The papers were duplicated in their original form and sent to 200 high schools. The teachers responsible for the first-year English course were requested to grade the papers using a 100-point scale, with a score of 75 being a passing grade.

Scored papers were returned from 142 of the schools. On one paper the scores varied from 64 to 98 points, with a mean of 88.2. The scores on the other paper ranged from 50 to 97, with a mean score of 80.2. The aura of objectivity that numbers gave to grading disappeared. The 47-point range was remarkable. As disturbing was the fact that one paper received 15 percent failing scores and 12 percent above 90.

Some subjectivity in grading English papers is understandable, but this amount was surprising. Starch and Elliot (1913) decided next to study subjectivity in scoring math papers. It would seem that scoring math papers would necessarily be much more objective. They repeated the study this time using a geometry paper.

They received 138 scored geometry papers. Surprisingly, the range of scores was even greater than they were on the English papers!

They found that chance could account for differences of four to seven points between two teachers grading the same paper and for the same teacher grading one paper on two different occasions.

From their statistical analysis, they concluded that it was practical to reliably score papers in broad increments. For instance, it was reliable to score papers as 95, 90, or 85 but not 95, 94, 93, etc. Additional research indicated that scales of five or ten points were about as many as could be reliably distinguished.

Letter grade scales and point scales, based on percentage equivalents from one to three or one to five, became increasingly popular. However, another problem was coming to the fore. This was the problem with how grades are or should be distributed. This was not a new problem; previously mentioned was the issue of grade inflation in the Virginia academy. The studies at about this time investigated the shape of grade curves. Some were found to be normal while others were found to be skewed in one direction or the other. Cureton (1971) recounts some of the issues and controversy that occurred around the turn of the century.

The system of grading that we call grading on the curve originated at the University of Missouri in about 1908. This system developed as a result of the hard grading of one professor who failed his whole class. The university's board overruled the professor and passed all the students. This incident prompted Meyer's classic paper of 1908 in which the system of grading on the curve as we now know it was outlined. He studied all of the grades given at the university and found no system or standard at all. He found that philosophy had the highest grades, chemistry the lowest, and psychology the middle. He pointed out all of the important uses of such undependable grades: for honors, admission to courses, repetition of courses, and dismissal from school. He felt that more science should be used in the administration of grades. Meyer's grading system put 50 percent of the students in the middle. This would greatly reduce the probability of unjust marking errors. He placed 22 percent in each of the categories he called inferior and superior, and 3 percent in each category he titled excellent and failures.

Further, Meyer recommended that the distribution of grades for each faculty member be published annually so that everyone could make comparisons. He also recommended that a faculty committee be appointed to supervise grading and keep the faculty in line. Meyer's system was soon adopted by a number of other colleges and universities.

Different distributions based on the curve were presented over the next decade. They differed according to shape and direction of skewness, but the system that we most commonly think of today was presented by Florian Cajori in 1914. He advocated the 7-24-38-24-7 distribution of grades. He also presented a table for normalizing scores (Cureton, 1971).

The introduction of the curve was an attempt to objectify grading and to protect students from capricious and arbitrary evaluation by their teachers. It was also an attempt to add some rigor to evaluation when instructors were being too generous in dispensing grades. Although this system did require that most of the students should do average or better, it made it desirable, even obligatory, that a portion of every group of students should be doing poor and failing work.

Even though the normal curve has become a popular concept, relatively few teachers actually use it. And, even though point scales and percentage grading systems had demonstrated lack of precision in the hands of unreliable measurers, they remained widely used and still are. Some teachers may apply a letter grade directly to a paper without first giving it a numerical score. This is more likely the case with written composition than it is with a spelling test or an arithmetic assignment. Usually, the paper will be checked and the number correct or incorrect tallied. It is here that point scores are converted to some form of grade. The teacher may calculate the distribution of grades. Some may do no more than calculate a mean and then make judgments about applying grades to scores that fall certain distances above and below it. A very few teachers may actually calculate a standard deviation or convert each score to a standard score so that it does fit in some place in a normal curve. In the latter cases, the grades assigned are likely to cover the complete range of 7-24-38-24-7.

In many other classrooms the teachers may not have the option of assigning grades according to a curve of any sort. Many teachers are obliged to assign grades according to a standard scale. The scales may be mandated on a system-wide basis or they may be the policy of individual schools or departments within schools. The following grading scale was adopted by the schools in Knox County, Tennessee, in 1988:

A: Excellent, 93–100 percent, regular; 88–100 percent, advanced placement.
B: Good, 85–92 percent, regular; 80–87 percent, advanced placement.
C: Average, 77–84 percent, regular; 75–79 percent, advanced placement.
D: Below Average, 70–76 percent, regular; 70–74 percent, advanced placement.
F: Failure, 0–69 percent, regular and advanced placement.
An A counts 4 points on a student's grade point average; B, 3 points; C, 2 points; and D, 1 point.

It is assumed that teachers will keep cumulative accounts of scores for each student and that when grades are to be issued the scores will be compared to the scale and a grade determined. This will be done without regard to any distribution of grades. Even though a C is called average, it is not an arithmetic average. It is simply an arbitrary point on the scale. It is possible, in a particular class, that a true mean of the scores or grades might be nowhere near the C grade given. The average score on a difficult test in science might be 55, for example. A teacher rigidly applying this grading scale would be required to fail most of the students taking it.

When such grading standards are used, the quality of evaluation methods are very important. When mean scores are in the failing range as in the above example, the content validity of the measuring methods must be deficient. Either they measured content that was not taught, or they were made up of poor or obscure items. Grading on curves was an attempt to remediate this problem. The C grades, or average grades, would be determined by the actual performance of a particular group rather than by an arbitrary standard. Average grades could not, by definition, be in the failing range. Grading scales, like the one from Knox County, assume that all measurement done by teachers is reliable, valid, and objective.

The grading systems that have evolved usually incorporate various scales and standards. The 100-point scale and a five-point letter-grade system are often used together. The location of the cutoff points for each grade can be considerably different, however. What should the lowest passing point be on such scales? Why is 70 often used as the lowest passing point? Why shouldn't we use 50 or even lower scores? Actually, many different passing points have been used. Nicolson (1917) reported that passing percentages for colleges of the time ranged from 20 percent to 70 percent.

The adoption of letter grades or similar point scales was an attempt to improve reliability and objectivity. Starch and Elliot felt that teachers could not reliably make judgments in less than about a seven-point error band. Consequently, grades were reported in more encompassing units. As in the Knox County scale, letter grades were assigned to seven-point ranges on the 100-point scale. Though this was an attempt to eliminate fine judgments with very imprecise instruments, fine judgments are still required. A single-point difference remains quite significant. Take, for example, the single point separating the 69 from 70. This is the difference between passing and failing. Should a single point in such unreliable systems really have this much influence? Single-point judgments are still required to differentiate between each of the letter grades. Granted, this is only true for scores that fall close to the boundaries, and really significant only for the student who happens to be on the less favorable side of it.

In recognition that not all classes are made up of students of the normal range of abilities, attempts have been made to be sensitive to these differences. In the Knox County classes that are for advanced placement, the scale is more generous at the A end. There is a 12-point range from 88 to 100 in which a student can get an A grade. The scale ranges narrow from seven points for a B to four points for a C or D. Failure is marked at the same cutoff point, 69, as for regular students. Many other schemes have been tried to assign grades based on different ability levels.

The need to determine different ability levels led to the development of the intelligence test. The Binet-Simon Scales appeared first in 1905 in France and were improved in 1908 and 1911 (Haney, 1984). In this country adaptions of the Binet-Simon scale were made, but the first thoroughly revised and standardized version of this test was the 1916 edition of the Stanford-Binet of Lewis Terman. Intelligence tests and testing became widely developed and widely used. The measurement of intelligence in the recruits for World War I gave great impetus to the considerable momentum the movement had attained before the war. After the war these instruments became widely used in schools.

The most popular use of such a test was for grouping students according to ability levels. This became a common practice during the 1920s (Cremin, 1961). Students in each grade were further graded into groups of slow, average, and rapid learners.

Standardized achievement tests appeared at about the same time and attained even more momentum in growth than IQ tests. These tests were developed to address the question of performance standards. These tests were to answer questions like, "What is average performance?" or "What is the desirable level of performance in any subject area?" If grades were to have any meaning they should stand for some objective behavior. From 1911 to 1919, standardized tests were developed for reading, writing, spelling, handwriting, etc. (Cureton, 1971). When norms became available from one of the tests, teachers were advised to try to bring their students up to at least the median score. The norms did show, however, that it was predictable and normal for students to fall far below the median performance at each age level.

Increased use of standardized tests prompted still more ability grouping. This brought about still more grading problems. Should the low-ability groups be given the same distribution of grades as the average- and high-ability groups (Smith & Dobbin, 1960)? Some recommended that A, B, and C be used for high-ability groups; B, C, and D for average; and C, D, and F for slower classes. Some advocated that the full range of grades be used with all ability groups. Some proposed that an additional symbol be used to mark the grades in order to show at which ability level the work was done.

Some negative effects of grading were noted in the 1930s (Smith & Dobbin, 1960). The incentive to cheat or overwork were cited. By the 1950s, considerable criticism was directed to grades because of the competitive basis for marking. Competitive grading was thought to be the reason for many antisocial attitudes and behaviors. Wrinkle (1947) suggested that elimination of competition in grading would make teachers rely on more acceptable methods of motivation and instruction. Recommendations emerged for grading based on student ability rather than on comparison and competition.

Studies of variability and reliability of grading were conducted again in the early fifties. It appeared that the change to A, B, C, D, F or their equivalents did little to make teachers more reliable in their grading practices. The studies dealt with the reliability of marks of the same teacher, from teacher to teacher in the same schools, and with grades assigned by different schools. Most teachers were found to differ on their interpretation of achievement. Grades differed from teacher to teacher and school to school. There was considerable discrepancy between grades teachers gave for achievement and scores on standardized achievement tests.

There were critics of grading on the scene while all this was going on. The progressive education movement had begun about the time the war had. Individual education plans were implemented. Students were to work at their own pace rather than move in lock step with a grade or group. Curriculum was assigned to individual students, not the reverse. There was a movement to abolish grades altogether. "Achievement must be individually gauged and therefore should not be graded comparatively." These systems advocated mastery learning approaches where the only important factor was whether or not a student had learned a skill and was therefore ready to move on. Some systems adopted pass-fail systems where the only distinction was between failing and acceptable work.

The systems of grading, grouping or classifying that had emerged by the end of the 1920s are pretty much those that exist today. There is an ebb and flow of interest in one area or another that still goes on. If there have been new developments, they have occurred in the area of measurement that produce still more classifications or grades of students. Witness the development of the learning disabilities classification and the myriad of tests that are used to classify children as such. This is the largest classification within special education today. There are attempts to further classify students even within this category. One recently added classification is the attention deficit disorder.

Tests and grades are used to classify children. They have virtually no use beyond this. Classification is primarily used for grouping and tracking which are themselves forms of grading which in turn reinforces the need for more testing and grading.

Testing for classification and to give grades provides no information that is specifically useful for instruction, but most testing done is precisely for these reasons. The fact that grades are used seems to legitimize failing a portion of students in every grade every year. We know that students will vary greatly on every trait measured. Since it is to be expected that students will vary as much as they do from average performance, why is it that the lower-performing students are given failing grades for performing in a way that should be expected? By what mythology can such a system be continued? That is the topic of the next chapter.

Chapter 3

MYTHS ABOUT GRADES

Grades emerged with free, public education. They are an institution. Their original meaning took on additional semantic baggage over the years, a meaning that has no basis in history or fact. A grand mythology is the foundation for their development and for their use. This mythology formed despite the critics who periodically complained almost from the beginning (Smith & Dobbin, 1960; Cureton, 1971).

Criticism of grades and the myths that sustain their use reached a peak in the 1970s. During this period works by Marshall (1968), Kirschenbaum, Napier, and Simon (1971), The National Education Association (1974), Simon and Bellanca (1976), and Bellanca (1977) highlighted the activity. Also during this time, a nonprofit educational agency (The National Center for Grading and Learning Alternatives) was founded. It was directed by James A. Bellanca. However, and unfortunately, after this peak period of activity, very little has been written on grading with the exception of an excellent book on grading at the college level (Milton, Pollio, & Eison, (1986).

I have concluded that we are at another critical juncture in the history of American education, where these myths have created some genuinely debilitating problems. Therefore, I feel it is necessary to review and expand on the problems that result from our mythology of grading.

There are many negative and destructive consequences that result from grades. Why do we persist in their use? It could only be because what we believe about grades contradicts these negative characteristics. These contradictory beliefs are our grade mythology. In this chapter I will describe the common myths and then summarize the contradictory facts for each.

In presenting these myths, I have not listed them in any order that should suggest to the reader any sense of priority. In other words, they are not listed in the order of how widely they are held or the order of their apparent distructiveness. They are simply listed randomly. The

21

reader will very likely recognize them all as commonly held beliefs about grades.

The first myth to be discussed has an element of truth in it. This is one reason that it remains a persisting belief. This myth is that grades are motivating. The element of truth in this myth is that grades are motivating to students if they get good grades.

It is believed that a poor grade will stimulate a student to do better work. However, there is no evidence to suggest this (Evans, 1976). Even for those students who are motivated by grades, the students who are already receiving good grades, there are some dark-side consequences. Anxiety is increased over fear of getting lower grades.

Students who get downgraded often continue to fail. It should be noted that poor grades and failure are not associated with productive learning activities. If a student is doing failing work, he is not getting the necessary productive practice to achieve better. Poor grades indicate poor practice and inadequate comprehension. Poor grades are more likely to be an indication of these conditions rather than a willing poor performance on the part of the student. When this is the case poor grades cannot be motivating; they will simply compound the problem. Poor grades will not make a student perform better if they are an indication that the work required of him is already too difficult.

Failure and failing grades are negatively motivating. They are likely to make a student feel helpless and ineffective. They contribute to the condition called "learned helplessness" by Grimes (1981). The effect of poor grades most often is to make students do worse. The increasingly poorer performance contrasts with the increasingly greater accomplishments of the high-achieving students. It is an instance of the rich get richer and the poor get poorer, but the riches are measured in terms of achievement. This phenomenon, as it occurs in the classroom, has been described as "Matthew effects" by Stanovich (1986). This phenomenon will be discussed in more depth in later chapters.

Through competition for the higher grades, grades are supposed to be motivating. Again, it is the students who are competitive, the students who already get good grades, that are motivated. Competition for the less able students is not motivating, it is demoralizing.

Grades are supposed to provide goals to strive for. For low-achieving students, however, good grades are placed well out of their reach. Being out of the students' reach produces the wrong kind of motivation. Students receiving poor grades, knowing they can't improve their lot through study, are motivated to cheat.

That grades provide goals is another myth. If we give this notion more than superficial consideration, we know that this isn't a proper goal. We know that learning is the proper goal of education. However, grades have become so confused with the educational process that learning has taken a secondary position. We seem to confuse grades with learning. As we do so, we teach students to work for grades and that learning is less important. Grades have become a more important objective of our educational system than learning. It is unfortunate that grades have become the goals, because they are unworthy ones.

Another myth is that grades are necessary for evaluation. Grades are supposed to tell us how much a student has learned. Actually, grades tell us nothing specific about how much or what a student has learned. They say nothing of strengths, weaknesses, readiness, deficits or achievement. Grades are only comparative or normative. They can show how a student is doing relative to his or her grade-level placement. They may show how the student is doing compared to other students in his or her classroom. They can show how well the students are matched to the instructional difficulty level of their placement.

They do not provide specific information that is useful in preparing instructional activities for individual students. They do not suggest what type of remedial help is needed by a student with a learning problem. They do not suggest where instruction should begin for a new student. In short, grades do not serve any instructionally useful purpose. Useful evaluation reveals specific information about where a student is on the scope and sequence of curricular objectives. It shows specifically what has been learned and what has not.

Even in the comparative or normative function, grades are unreliable indicators. Teachers vary greatly in their grading practices, from extremely generous to quite difficult. This is true grade by grade, subject by subject, within the same school, and from school to school. Standardized, norm-referenced achievement tests are better at this function. Reasonably accurate comparisons can be made of a student's performance to others in his or her classroom or in similar circumstances elsewhere. Comparisons are only limited by the amount of normative information available for each achievement test. Standardized achievement tests have the same limitation as grades, however, in regard to the fact that they do not reveal useful instructional information (Shriner & Salvia, 1988; Hargis, 1987).

Another myth is that grades are objective. Grades are not reliable; consequently, they are not objective. The variability of grades assigned by different teachers was just discussed. This variability exists even when teachers are using the same grading system (Smith & Dobbin, 1960). There are many extraneous variables that affect grades. The sex of the teacher and the sex of the student are both factors that influence the grades assigned. Personal characteristics such as appearance or how well students are liked influence grading.

The socioeconomic area a school serves will have considerable influence on what a grade means. An "A" in a wealthy suburban school will mean something quite different from an "A" in a poor inner-city school. It is almost necessary to have a zip code along with grades to make even a rough interpretation of what they mean.

The lack of reliability among teachers has been mentioned. Moreover, teachers are not consistent in the marks they themselves assign. Also, there are discrepancies between grades assigned by teachers to specific students and the scores received by the same students on standardized achievement tests.

Despite the lack of reliability and objectivity of grades, they are used to make decisions that can have enormous impact on students. Failing grades are really our primary diagnostic tool for identifying candidates for special education or other special service. High grades are used to identify students for certain honors or to screen them for special programs for the academically talented.

We think grades are essential for screening students for college admission. The fact is that colleges cannot rely on grades alone to predict how qualified students are for matriculation. This is true at many schools, particularly those that have rigorous academic curricula. Colleges and universities typically require more objective measures of academic achievement progress. They require scores from tests such as the SAT or ACT in order for a student to be considered for admission. Most colleges will admit students without "grade" transcripts. They simply require more information such as SAT/ACT test results, other achievement test scores, written teacher evaluation, criterion lists, or essays (Bellanca, 1977).

Besides these myths, tradition also seems to be a force that perpetuates the use of grades. We have always had grades, and we know no other means of getting feedback on what is going on in school. This feedback is better than no feedback. Our institutions have, over the three generations of their widespread use, neither retained nor developed substantive methods of reporting achievement progress.

"What was good enough for me is good enough for my children." "I had to endure grades when I was in school. My kids can tough them out, too." We feel that grades are like life. Getting graded is simply preparation for life's competitive, dog-eat-dog trials.

Grades have become a student's responsibility. They are something to be worked for. If a student doesn't get good grades, then it is his responsibility to work harder. Grades place students in competition with each other. They set up competitive environments in classrooms that do not foster learning. They isolate students from each other. Students are supposed to do their own work and work for their own grade. Cooperative activity is discouraged despite massive evidence that shows how much it facilitates learning and achievement. Grades have become such an important end that less competitive students are often forced to cheat in order to get a passing grade or to get a grade that prevents bringing down the wrath of their parents.

More humane teachers, recognizing the potential harm that grades can cause, are likely to be reluctant to give students poor grades, especially if they see the students are making an attempt to do the work. In the process of giving higher grades, the humane teachers are distorting the distribution of grades and contributing to so-called "grade inflation."

Teachers who are generous in the grades they award are likely to feel some criticism for not maintaining academic standards. They are not being tough enough on their students. It is as if a normal distribution of grades is evidence of some admirable teaching quality.

It certainly seems to me that this is the opposite of what should be the attitude about grades. If grades are evidence of how much is learned, then the evidence of good teaching and learning must be good grades. If teachers are truly good, then the students will be learning well; and if they are learning well, then they must get good grades. It would seem to me to be evidence that good teaching is going on when the bulk of the students under a teacher's care get good grades. This should warrant praise. However, it is likely to be viewed as grade inflation, and the teacher is likely to be accused of low standards.

A normal distribution of grades should not be considered as evidence of good teaching. Standards should not really even be associated with a grading system. A normal distribution of grades is primary evidence that a teacher who is assigning the grades is not attending instructionally to the individual differences of his or her students. A normal distribution of grades is produced when one level of instruction is provided to a group of students, and they all have the same amount of instructional time devoted to it.

Having grades and being expected to give a wide distribution of them actually makes teachers disregard individual differences. It shifts the responsibility for achievement from the teacher to the student. It is the students' responsibility to study harder, to try harder in every way to get better grades.

Another insidious myth about grades is that tests should be administered in order to grade. The weekly tests, the six-week test, the term test, the final test, whatever the name, they all must be used to find grades. Most testing is done for the purpose of giving grades. Grade books are filled with the results of quizzes and tests.

Contradicting this use of testing is the notion that tests should be used to provide helpful feedback to students. Tests should be used to find out what additional instruction a student may need, to see if the student has mastered instructional objectives, or to find out where a student is so instruction can fruitfully begin at an appropriate difficulty level. Grades are the end product of most assessment. Helpful feedback should, however, be the objective of most assessment. Grades are not specific. With grades, a teacher is not compelled to provide specific feedback. Without specific information about what is wrong, students are kept demoralized and confused. Testing should be a part of the instructional process, not apart from it.

When testing is separate from the instructional process and used for giving grades, teachers will be getting little information on what the individual needs of students are. Errors become simply red marks to be tallied, summed, averaged and entered in a grade book. About the only feedback possible under these conditions is that the student is doing fine, alright, or he had better do better.

Grades require errors. In order to get a distribution of grades, there must be a range in the number of errors. Teachers may even make tests harder, more discriminating, in order to insure that some students will make enough mistakes so they will get a good grade distribution. This further removes tests from the instructional process. Students often complain that, "That test was too hard. You didn't have that in class. That wasn't in the book."

When testing is used for giving grades, test results are not immediately acted upon. Students should be getting immediate helpful feedback to see specifically what they need to improve or practice. Without quick feedback, students are at risk for practicing errors. They have the opportunity to learn mistakes. This results in the need for remedial help.

Instruction will proceed along at the single pace without regard to what individual students are experiencing, if tests are used primarily for grades. Tests should be used to modify instructional difficulty or to adjust the instructional pace for students. Testing for grades virtually precludes this. If testing was used for providing feedback and for modifying instruction, grades, of necessity, would go up. This form of complementary teaching and testing insures that instruction is delivered in a way that produces fruitful learning in each student. Testing for grades virtually requires that instruction not be modified. This is so since a distribution of scores is required. In this way some students will do well and thereby get excellent grades, some will do poor and failing work, and the bulk will do the average work and get average grades.

When we organize instruction around grade levels, we operate under an assumption which is actually a myth. We believe that by grouping by chronological age and by ability we have made sufficient concession to the ranges of individual differences of students. In doing this we feel that we should be able to provide one level of instruction. We believe that we have compressed the range of learning needs sufficiently so that one level of instruction can be used; a set of instructional material with the same difficulty level can be provided; and the same instructional pace can be maintained. The fact that most children can succeed in this system and make reasonable achievement progress perpetuates this organizational system. Nevertheless, the fact that about a quarter of our students don't fit these grading organizations and do not succeed is grim testimony to the mythical nature of our present grading and grouping practices.

There always remains remarkable variation in the individual learning abilities of students no matter how carefully they are grouped. When given one level of instruction, the range in scores and grades that results is testimony to this variation. The nature and extent of these individual differences is the subject of the next chapter.

Chapter 4

NORMAL VARIATION IN ACADEMIC ABILITY

We expect and accept wide differences among individuals in various human traits. We assume as normal, marked variation in physical characteristics such as height, body mass, temperature sensitivity, eye-hand coordination, foot speed, strength, and endurance. We believe that musical or artistic talent, mechanical, social or athletic aptitude exist in wide ranges. Nevertheless, we are quite insensitive to the range of individual differences in academic aptitude that exists in every group of students.

It is actually more than just an insensitivity to individual differences in academic talent; we all too often view the wider differences as maladies which need to be cured. The extent and consequences of this problem, as well as the reasons for our intolerance of individual differences in academic ability, are explored in this chapter.

Actually, extremes in normal variation of many kinds can appear to be a problem depending on the setting. The setting, however, will be designed according to some normative standard. Possibly the most commonly encountered of such standards are building codes and the standards used in designing public and private conveyances. These standards govern things like the height and width of door openings, the height and depth of counter tops, the placement of kitchen shelves and cabinets, bed and furniture sizing, and the leg room and seat sizes for airlines, buses, and automobiles. These are examples of just a few of the common standards that we encounter daily. These standards are certainly no problem for the "average" person. This means that about two-thirds of the adult population will encounter no discomfort or inconvenience because of these standards. However, the persons taller than six feet two inches will begin to have problems depending on how much they exceed the standard. Problems of a different sort will be encountered by persons shorter than about five feet two inches because they are also out of the tolerance limits imposed by these standards. The normal height distribution ranges from about four feet six inches to about seven feet four inches. Some standards handicap both ends of the distribution, some only one. For example, bed length handicaps only the tall. On the other hand, either extreme in foot width, 5E or 5A, can make it extremely difficult to find shoes that fit. Academic aptitude is like foot width: either extreme has a problem fitting into school.

How much normal variation is there in any age group or grade? This question must be raised in terms of age groups and grades because they provide the outline of the standard into which students must fit. In each classroom the age range of students is at least one year. This age range is established when students are admitted to kindergarten or first grade. In order to begin the lock-step sequence of grades, children must have reached their fifth or sixth birthday by an established date sometime during the fall of that school year. If a student's birthdate is on that day, say October fifteenth, he will be admitted and will be among the youngest members of his class. If, however, a student's birthdate falls even one day after the cutoff, he will wait until the next year to begin the lock-step progression. Then the student will be among the oldest members of his class. So, we find the twelve-month range in age that is built into each classroom. This is an administrative procedure, which is used to mass manage large numbers of students in our school systems. Even though this is an attempt to group students according to similar age and, therefore, what are assumed to be similar readiness levels, it is not particulary effective. Consider the fact that children in the extremes of the chronological age range in any classroom are as close in age to about as many students in the grade either above or below them as they are to students in their own grade. The assumption, then, would be that their academic readiness would be closer as well.

Actually, chronological age is a poor indication of academic aptitude or readiness. It is, however, the primary gauge we use. There are a variety of measures, including readiness tests, achievement tests, and teacher judgments, that give far better indications of the extent of academic aptitude. The range in chronological age which does give a coarse indication of maturity, especially at the primary and elementary grade levels, interacts with actual differences in academic aptitude to produce very great differences in achievement in every classroom. While chronological age segregation may give an impression of homogenous grouping, a remarkable range of educationally critical differences still exist.

Normal differences per se should not be problems, or worse, handicaps. However, normal differences can be handicaps when they are out of tolerance with the standards and norms used to build structures into which they must be. We seldom appreciate the inflexibility and the limited tolerance that the grade level structure of schools and their lock-step curriculum have.

Instructional materials are designed to follow sequences of skills in various subject areas that make up the curriculum. Material and objectives appropriate for average students are assigned to each grade level. This is apportioned and sequenced over the approximately 178 days that make up the school year. This apportionment allows sufficient time for the average range of students to learn the content, or at least pass through the year without failing. Still, every year, in almost every classroom a quarter of the students are doing very poor or failing work. For the most part, the reason for this is that these students are out of tolerance with the standards and norms of their classrooms.

I have mentioned the inevitable variation in chronological age at each grade; the normal variation that exists in actual achievement among students in every classroom is far greater. This evidence is available from the normative data on any popular achievement test. This information reflects the actual ranges of achievement found in each grade level in large representative samples of students throughout the country. I am going to illustrate the normal extent of the individual differences in reading achievement to be found in the primary grades by referring to the norms of the *Peabody Individual Achievement Test,* the 1970 edition.

RANGES IN ACHIEVEMENT

	1st	2nd	3rd	4th
Scores	60–160	80–225	105–260	129–285
Grades	0.5–3.4	1.1–5.3	1.9–7.1	2.5–8.7

The range in achievement reported in this illustration excludes the bottom and top 5 percent of the students in each grade. In other words the ranges reported go from the fifth to the ninety-fifth percentile of scores and grade equivalents for these scores at each grade level. This removal was done to insure that most of the mildly handicapped students were eliminated from the bottom portion of the distribution (Stone, Cundick, & Swanson, 1988) and that the academically talented or gifted students were removed from the other end of the continuum.

I want to reemphasize that this represents the range of academic ability that teachers in typical first through fourth grade classrooms across the country confront. Notice that while the range in chronological age may be restricted to a single year, the range in actual reading achievement is many times greater! The range in reading achievement at the end of the first grade is 2.9 years, at the end of the second grade, 4.2 years, at the end of the third grade, 5.2 years, and at the end of the fourth grade, 6.2 years. Another way of looking at these figures is to examine the change in range in each succeeding grade. From the end of the first grade to the end of the fourth grade the range in reading achievement will more than double.

We know that we are often misled by statistics. In the case of achievement statistics we usually mislead ourselves. We confuse average with normal. Even though the range in actual achievement in each grade is normally wide and normally becomes wider in each successive grade, the average remains the same single year point, each point spaced exactly one year from the adjacent grades. The average figure for each grade is a mask for the normal, wide range of individual differences that exists in each grade and actually widens each year. The average for each grade becomes the standard for achievement. We even have come to think that it is abnormal for students to be performing below this average grade level standard. The fact is, however, that it is normal for students in every grade to achieve considerably less than the average standard.

It is also normal for students to learn at different rates. That is precisely why the range in achievement widens at each successive grade level. The student at the fifth percentile rank of achievement learns at a rate about 40 percent slower than the average student. He makes about .6 of a year's progress each year. On the other hand, the student at the ninety-fifth percentile rank learns about 40 percent faster than the average and makes about 1.8 years' progress in reading achievement each year. The range in learning rates is seldom appreciated. The curriculum structure provides no attention to the extremes of learning rate or the marked variation in the need for repetition and practice before mastery of each objective is attained. Again, the rate of introduction and repetition is satisfactory for most students but certainly is not for the slower learners in each grade.

Unlike the range in chronological age, the range in achievement always extends far beyond the grade level boundaries in both directions. It is not unnatural for students to be achieving one or more grade levels below or above actual grade placement. It is normal and to be expected. However, we do not treat below average performance as normal. We view normal, below average performance as a malady which should be cured. Below average performance is as normal as above average performance.

Achievement that is below a student's potential for achievement, not the class average, should be the point of concern. We should be primarily attentive to making sure that all students are doing as well as they can. We should expect markedly varied achievement in every classroom. We cannot prepare useful educational goals for students by using average grade-level performance in the formulation. At any rate, we should always start work with students at their current performance level. We cannot realistically expect to make achievement progress by making students work at the average curricular level of their grade placement. If their achievement level is below it, they will likely fail.

Our notion of instruction is so tied to the curricular content assigned to a given grade that most teachers will not or cannot provide instruction that matches the various levels of achievement in their classrooms. Evidence of the extent to which teachers are able to match the level of instruction with the various achievement levels of students in their rooms is the distribution of grades assigned. A wide distribution of grades shows that there is only the single level of instruction from the curriculum assigned to that grade. The lower-achieving students in the room will get the poor and failing grades. The higher-achieving students will get the A's and B's.

If every student in the room were given work to do that was appropriate to his or her level of actual achievement rather than the work that was assigned to their grade, every student would demonstrate about the same level of performance. In other words, if a student is given work that fits his or her current level of achievement, then that student would be doing that work well and getting a good or at least an acceptable grade. On the other hand, if a teacher adheres strictly to the curriculum assigned to that grade and gives every student the same level of work to do, the students whose achievement level is below that of the assigned work will get the poor grades, and the students whose achievement level is at or above that of the assigned work will get the acceptable to high grades.

A complete range of grades, which mirrors the achievement distribution of the students in the room, will be produced if only grade-level curriculum and instruction is provided. When teachers assign a normal distribution of grades to their students, they provide direct evidence that they are not attending to the individual differences in achievement of their students. These teachers are only providing grade-level instruction. If some students can't do the work, well, that is just too bad.

The structure of schools is such that it is administratively convenient to assign students and curriculum to the lock-step sequence of grades. The attempt to match curriculum difficulty to student ability has been done through sequencing the hierarchy of skills through succeeding grades. However, one can readily see that the assignment of students to grades by chronological age standards leaves too many students outside the tolerance limits. Consequently, the students that fall too far below the tolerance limits of their grades fail. Every year, in almost all classrooms, several students are failing. They are simply out of tolerance limits of the lock-step curriculum in the grades where they are.

Since we seem bound by the need to provide one level of instruction to students, we try to manage individual differences among the students through ability grouping or tracking. We try to organize students so they fit within the tolerance limits of curriculum content being presented at each grade step. Consequently, virtually all of our procedures for dealing with student variability involve grouping and tracking. We are very resistant to reorganizing the curriculum and our teaching system so that it can be fitted to the individual needs of students. We always do the reverse. We try to fit the students to the grade and curriculum structure.

The scope of grouping and tracking practices that go on depend on the size of the school and school system. However, even in individual elementary classrooms, teachers will have divided their students into three or more reading groups: the fast, average, and slow groups. When the schools are large enough to have more than one class at each grade level, the students will be divided by ability again, with further grouping going on within each classroom. All this grouping is done so that one level of instruction can be provided to the whole group. It is a fitting procedure. It is done to fit students into the rigid curricular structure. Still, students do not fit. Those who do not, fail and fall further and further behind their own potential for achievement.

Even some academically talented students may find themselves in conflict with the tolerance limits of the curriculum assigned to their grade or group. However, the problem is more obvious when it concerns the low-achieving student. Here, the child encounters materials and instructional activities that are too difficult for him and he can't do the work. Not being able to do the work, he can't make himself attend to it for any length of time, so he will be off task. This nonattending behavior can get him into trouble and even get him labeled as having a short attention span, or worse, as having an attention deficit disorder or as being hyperdistractible. With the academically talented student, the curricular content and the instructional activities may be too easy. They may seem like boring busywork. These students may avoid the work and demonstrate some of the same off-task behavior that the low-achieving students do. These students are often out of the tolerance limits of the curriculum as well.

Arranging students to fit curricular structures seldom works completely. Some professional schools, though, do such a thorough job of screening out candidates that do not fit that they consequently have very high success rates. However, our public schools are obligated to take all students and educate them to the maximum extent possible. This cannot be done with low-achieving students simply by grouping them. The curriculum must be assigned with appropriate flexibility to individual students so that they can make the best achievement progress they can without becoming a casualty of intolerant curriculum boundaries.

We devote enormous energies to grouping, tracking, and classifying children to fit them into some curricular slot. A lot of the energy is devoted to classifying students who are failing so that they can be grouped for some special assistance or service. We have an immense number of tests that are used to figure out why students fail. These tests typically are aimed at producing a label to place on the student so that he can be placed in a group with others that share the same problem. We have so many tests, some of which require special training to administer, that we have employed many specialists just to administer them and interpret the results.

We have such faith in the sanctity of the curriculum and grade-level structure that we have lost our tolerance of individual differences in learning ability and facility. All students must conform to the curriculum and grade structures. The extent that they do conform to their assigned position is measured by the range of grades given to them. However, we do not view the distribution of grades as an assessment of fit. We view the poor grades as a student problem. It is the students' fault that they get poor grades. Barring this interpretation, it is a problem or disability within the students that produces the failure. We will almost never diagnose failure as a faulty curriculum match.

The fact that we have a range of grades to give legitimizes giving the complete range. We somehow feel obligated to do so. Grades have somehow come to be associated with standards. The only way we feel we can show that we are maintaining standards is by making sure that we don't give too many high grades. The distribution of abilities that will occur in most groups of students will produce a similar distribution of grades given one level of instruction. We may even think that it is good to give a wide distribution of grades and that good teachers are hard graders. Remember, however, that when a teacher gives a wide distribution of grades, that distribution is produced by providing instruction of only one difficulty level. Moreover, teachers who give mostly low grades have provided work above the appropriate instructional level of most of the students in their charge. When the match is made between the instructional difficulty level and the current instructional-level ability of a student, the student's performance will necessarily be good so as to indicate the match has been made. Teachers who carefully attend to this match are truly attending to the individual difference of their students. The performance levels of the students will necessarily be similar, though the instructional activities and materials will be of various levels. It is very difficult to use conventional grades if this is done.

Chapter 5

THE LOCK-STEP CURRICULUM

The sum of the topics that make up the course of study in a school is its curriculum. We can think of it simply as a list of the content and skills that a school plans to teach. Some topics require developmental treatment that extends over several years. Reading and arithmetic are such topics. The course of study for each of these topics is organized according to a hierarchy of skills. The aggregate of skills and subtopics are laid out in a sequence reflecting the developmental order. In reading and arithmetic, the scope and sequence of topics and skills covers eight or more school years. Other course work is placed in the curriculum according to its order of difficulty. Some course work may be prerequisite and so courses are ordered according to readiness requirements. For example, chemistry courses require math course work and so will be placed in the curricular sequence after math. The general order and content for most public school curricula are quite similar.

The scope and sequence of skills, topics, and courses that make up a school's curriculum must fit within the school calendar, twelve or thirteen nine-month increments. Only a certain amount of time can be devoted to each item before moving on to the next. All of the students assigned to any given grade or classroom must cover the same topics in the same order before moving on to the next. The topics assigned to that course or grade must be covered before that year is over. This must be done so that the students can be ready to continue on to the next curricular step the next year.

The organization of the curriculum is in lock step. The steps are ordered by the calendar. Each year forms a large step, but there are many substeps as well. School systems vary, but generally the steps are defined by testing and grading periods. The system has large lock steps and small lock steps. All of the students entering must move through the system in lock-step unison.

At the elementary level, the curricular items have been assigned to each small lock step by normative standards. This is done, not by a formal normative process, but by experience and trial and error over many years. The curricular demands for each level have worked out to be reasonable for most students. The amount of material covered and the threshold of difficulty must permit the majority of students to proceed along the curricular path in unison. The threshold must be low enough for the majority to achieve. Consequently, it will be well below the threshold achievement levels of the abler students. Still, high achievers must pace themselves according to the same normative lock step.

The most direct, however controversial, procedure for dealing with the highest-achieving students is acceleration. It is a procedure for breaking the lock step. High-achieving students are permitted to move through the curriculum at an accelerated pace. This includes practices like grade skipping, compressing course work, or testing out of courses in which the students have already mastered the content. Accelerated students, in this way, are helped to achieve at their own natural pace through the curriculum. Their progress is not retarded by requiring them to maintain the lock-step pace through the curriculum.

I mentioned that this was a controversial practice. It is not permitted in many school systems. Gifted students are quite often required to take the prescribed number of lock steps over the same time frame.

Low-achieving students, those whose achievement threshold is below that of their age group's grade level, will not be able to maintain the pace. They will fall further and further behind. Failure and lack of achievement will cause them to repeat a grade—retaking a large lock step. This is an attempt to help them get in step. Even decceleration for these students will be done in lock step for the most part.

The curricular lock step has become a normative yardstick. A student's performance is gauged against the normative measure of the difficulty of the material assigned to each grade and step. Performance against this normative measure is reported with grades. The lock-step curriculum, in fact, is largely responsible for having grades. Grades are really only a device by which students can be compared to the normative standard of each curriculum lock step.

The yardstick use of the curriculum reinforces the use of grades. Grades, in turn, reinforce the use of the single level of instruction assigned to each step of the curriculum which is also assigned to each calendar unit. One level of instruction produces the distribution of grades which we have come to accept and to respect. The largest portion of the students are supposed to get passing grades, and they will if this number of students has the ability to deal with the demands of the curriculum topic assigned to the class they are in.

In recognition of the fact that some course work or subject areas are too difficult for some students, alternative curricular tracks have been developed. This has led to the practice of ability grouping. Still, when the students are regrouped according to ability, they find themselves in courses with a single level of instruction. A distribution of grades is still expected. In classrooms and courses where academically talented students are grouped together, the need to produce a distribution of grades may be unfair and cause unreasonable, stressful competition. Excellent performance may be unfairly rated simply because it will be ranked next to even more excellent performance.

With ability grouping, we find that students who would receive excellent grades in the mainstream will get only average grades. And students who were only average in ungrouped situations now receive high grades. It is often observed that grades awarded in systems with ability grouping are unfair, not necessarily to the students, but to the spirit of the grading system! Critics say grading this way lacks meaning unless the grade is noted along with the group status of the class in which it was received.

Curricular paths diverge but each remains lock step. Tracking was developed in an attempt to better deal with individual differences, and to some extent it does reach more students by permitting them to follow tracks more geared to their particular needs. However, the curriculum for each track is still assigned to grades and calendar units. Ability levels in each classroom varies considerably even though the broader range of abilities has been subdivided into two or more tracks. The range in abilities is still enough to produce a distribution of grades as the different students work with the same instructional level of material.

If the ability range of the students is narrowed sufficiently that they all fall within the same performance limits, their performance may in fact be remarkably similar. Teachers in this case find themselves in a dilemma. They may feel compelled to give all the students the same grade and at the same time to give a normal range of grades. Situations like this do exist when the ability level of the students is well above the threshold for top grades. All of the students may get 96 percent and above on their assignments and tests and so qualify for A's. Teachers who feel the need to give a more nearly normal range of grades to such students may become more "picky" in the way they grade assignments and tests. They may also try to make their assignments and tests more difficult and discriminating in order to produce the desired distribution of grades. These practices seldom have anything to do with learning, and they may well demoralize a good many students.

Students whose achievement level is at or above the threshold requirement for passing work in their curricular track are safe from failure and can expect to make reasonable progress. If they are not quite up to this threshold, they will be in trouble. In elementary and intermediate grades, failure will mean retention or consideration for special education evaluation. If the student does not appear to qualify for special education by any standards, then he will, in all liklihood, be required to repeat the grade. Students with learning abilities that keep them out of pace with the cadence required to keep in step with their school's curriculum will be required to get in step or get special help.

The procedure for attempting to get students in step with the curriculum is restarting them at a lower level, repeating a grade. If it turns out that a student has some disability that makes it unlikely that he can get in step with the curriculum cadence by repeating grades, then he will be placed in another track, the special education track.

For some students, repeating grades will be sufficient for getting them within the tolerance limits of a curricular slot and for making adequate achievement. There are, however, a great many normal, low-achieving students who will get little if any relief from repeating grades, and if there is relief it is usually temporary. The lower-achieving students may require 50 percent more time than their average peers to learn the same material. Repeating a grade is only a temporary fix. The curricular cadence will go on. The lower-achieving student's slower pace will gradually let him fall behind once more. Eventually, he will be out of the tolerance limits of his curricular level and he will fail again.

Students that drop out very often have experienced these problems. They will have failed and will have been retained for one or more grades. In high school, they will have fallen sufficiently far behind so that they will lack the readiness requirements to enter and perform in much of the course work. Experiencing little success and with little prospect for doing so, they drop out.

Students who are out of synchronization with the pace of the lock-step curriculum are the source of most of the variation in grades. The academically able learners will usually get the highest grades or have the highest test scores, while the less able will get the poorest grades and scores. The use of lock-step curricula virtually assures that a normal distribution of grades can be obtained from any randomly chosen age group of students.

Such a distribution of grades will be obtained, even with excellent teaching, as long as the teaching is focussed on that one level prescribed by the curriculum for that group of students. A distribution of grades is the inevitable and natural consequence of the lock-step curriculum. Single-level, teacher-centered instruction is also the standard because of it. Students are expected to fit in their assigned slot. Teachers are supposed to organize their instruction around the set of topics assigned to the slot in the curriculum for which they are responsible. Grades are supposed to be assigned in a wide distribution, otherwise they would not mean anything. So go the stereotypes created by our curricular organization.

We also stereotype our expectations for student performance based on their age and grade placement. We expect students to be able to perform the curricular tasks assigned to that age and grade. We are reluctant to accept the fact that it is normal to achieve at levels either far above or far below age and grade norms. Neither are we willing to accept the consequences of our attempts to make students conform to our stereotypes.

Commercially prepared instructional materials dominate curricular content. These commercial instructional materials also dictate the scope and sequence of skills to be taught and the rate at which they are presented. In short, they form the very basis of K through twelve curricula.

Commercial basal reading and math programs virtually control the form of the reading and mathematics curricula in elementary schools. Publishing companies prepare these developmental programs to cover first through the sixth or eighth grades. They spell out in detail exactly what is to be presented in the classroom for each and every day of each school year. The teacher's presentation and even the instructional talk to be used are provided in the teacher's manuals. Every one of the students in any given classroom will have textbooks and workbooks with activities to work at independently in school and at home.

The instructional program for each subsequent year picks up where the previous one left off. With developmental instructional programs such as basal math and reading series, the scope and sequence of skill covers the school year day by day and then the grades year by year. At the secondary grade levels, some subject areas are fairly isolated, like algebra, history, chemistry. In these cases textbooks will be available that cover the content over one year's time only.

It should be noted that at any grade level in any class or subject all of the books are the same. They will likely have the readability level of the norm for that grade. The workbooks and the activities are identical, too. There may be some minor suggestion for enrichment activities and some suggestion for supplementary activities for students that vary from the single level of instruction. Most of these programs have assessment devices for testing learning and mastery. They provide these measuring devices to see how well the students keep pace with their program and to grade them accordingly.

These material are part and parcel of the lock-step curriculum. They are organized to fit the lock step and they clearly reinforce its continued use. They provide the uniform level of instructional material and activities that assures a wide distribution of grades.

A considerable portion of anthropological study is devoted to the cultural phenomenon, the rites of passage. Since the advent of compulsory education, our schools have largely taken on the function of providing the rites of passage. Schools are the common dominating force in the life of children, from the toddler age through puberty to adulthood.

The curriculum marks the stages of childhood and defines the transition points. Schools provide the rituals to verify that students are moving toward entry in the adult community. The rituals are the graduation ceremonies that occur at varies grade levels.

The lock-step curriculum requires grades, and grades provide the students with the evidence needed to make the passage. Passing grades are fundamental to fulfilling a rite of passage. Each stage, a grade or a course, can be viewed as a stage to be passed; passing grades are passing rites.

Failing grades and courses are very disruptive to students because they are important to a child's need to achieve the rites of passage. It is troublesome that all these rites now are largely academically based, based on a system that is guaranteed to deny passing rites to a significant number of students.

Denial of the rites of passage is for many students, in my opinion, disruptive and disintegrative. They may seek ways of verifying their own passage through childhood through modeling nonacademic behavior that represents characteristics of members of the stage to which they aspire. If the characteristics are negative, so much the worse for the low-achieving student. It is the fortunate student who is durable enough to leave the system unfulfilled and enter the adult community as a reasonable productive member.

The lock-step curriculum is doubtless an administratively efficient way of dealing with large numbers of students. It permits instructional methods and materials to be developed and supplied very efficiently. It very much resembles an assembly-line process. After all, the system emerged in parallel with our industrialization. Students move through each step in the assembly process and come out with the standard measures of equipment. That is, they do if they can fit the standard mold. Clearly, at least 25 percent do not fit and so fall in the reject pile before the assembly line ends. A significant number of others may be rolled out at the end of the process but are still labeled inferior products.

The defects and shoddiness of the educational assembly line results from our attempts to make students conform to the tolerance limits of the lock-step curriculum. Our grading system is really only the gauge we use to measure the extent that students do or do not fit. There is really only one remedy to this situation: we must stop trying to make students fit the curriculum structure. This simply produces defects and shoddiness in those that don't fit. What we must do is adjust the curriculum pace to fit the student. Simply put, the curriculum should be fitted to students, not the reverse. The evidence of the fit will be in work done well and work that merits high scores or grades. The evaluation will concern the quality of the match that has been made between student and the instructional level of the curricular placement.

Individual differences in achievement will always exist. We cannot cure them by making students conform to the performance standard dictated by each step in the lock-step curriculum. In the attempt to make students conform, we cause students' achievement to fall further and further behind their personal potentials. Failing grades are primary evidence that this negative process is in action.

Chapter 6

THE SPECIALIST SYSTEM

Lock-step curricula isolate curriculum content in specific grades and courses. Teachers assigned to specific grades or courses must specialize in teaching the subject matter that goes with their assignment. Teachers fit slots on the curriculum; teacher training and certification emphasizes such specialization. Education, like business and industry, is increasingly dominated by specialists.

Teachers seem to develop a proprietary relationship with the curricular content in their particular niche. They are encouraged to do so. Their supervisors and administrators emphasize the importance of covering and completing all items assigned to their grade or course in the prescribed time. Teachers, therefore, of necessity, specialize in teaching and become responsible for a proscribed and particular set of curricular items.

The focus of instruction is on getting material covered. Instruction becomes curriculum centered rather than student centered. Teachers must keep up the curriculum pace. They must get through the material assigned to their grade or course in order to get the students ready for the next curricular lock step with its specialist teacher. There is little mind given to the fact that students are not keeping up the pace. The beat must go on.

If students are not able to benefit from the instruction provided in the specialist teacher's classroom, it is either the students' fault or the fault of the previous teacher who failed to get the students ready to pick up the pace of instruction.

We know that the actual range of achievement of students in any grade overlaps that of the students in the grades both above and below. Despite this knowledge, the specialist system causes teachers to view this normal variation as anomalous. They either avoid conceding it exists or view it as a defect in the student or as the result of inadequate teaching. The thinking of the specialist is so dominated by the curriculum component in their charge that instruction seldom deviates from the precisely laid out instructional plan for the school year. All efforts at individualization will be directed to the curriculum content, not the students' individual achievement levels. The specialist may recognize that significant numbers of students are not learning well and, in an effort to reach them, present the content through a variety of learning styles. Alternatively, the instructor may vary his or her presentation by using such things as Socratic methods rather than lecture, or by introducing humor and entertainment. Content may be packaged in a variety of media. It will, however, invariably be the same specialized curriculum.

The extent to which the difficulty level of the instruction and materials that a student encounters in any course or grade matches the actual ability levels of the students will be reflected by the range of grades and scores received by the students. The number of poor and failing grades is largely a measure of this mismatch.

The boundaries between grades and courses are sharply drawn in the lock step. Teachers often feel an isolated duty to their place on the curriculum. The fact that some students don't do well or fail is not their responsibility. They are the keeper of the standards of the curriculum. If some students fail as a result of maintaining the standard, then the problem is one of the students and is the purview of some other specialist who is supposed to handle such things.

In the elementary grades, teachers typically specialize in teaching the entire curriculum content of a grade. In other words, a teacher will teach all the subject areas, reading, writing, math, science, etc., but only for a single grade level. Teachers typically prepare for a somewhat wider range of grades but, upon employment, settle on a single grade. At higher grade levels, specialization becomes even more narrow.

By about the seventh grade, students move from class to class, teacher to teacher. Teachers are responsible for certain subjects. All of the students in a school may rotate through their classrooms. A teacher now is responsible for teaching all the students the same subject, while in earlier grades, a teacher was responsible for teaching all the subjects to only one group of children. The specialist teacher will often have well over a hundred different students in their classrooms each day.

In such impersonal environments, teachers cannot attend to the individual needs of students. The individual awareness of their students seldom can go much beyond learning their names. Grading tests and papers with such large numbers of students takes great amounts of time, and that is true even if only a minute or two is devoted to each paper.

Instruction is extremely difficult to individualize when such large numbers of students are encountered every day. Virtually all testing is done only for the purpose of giving grades. These grades are simply normative gauges of how the many students are doing given the single grade-level instruction provided in each of the specialist's classes. The specialist feels an obligation to the course content. The specialist teacher's duty to the students seldom goes beyond scoring their tests and papers and giving them a grade.

There are some who argue for teacher specialization. However, I feel most of their arguments are inadequate. There is even some interest in moving the specialist system down further into the elementary grades. Advocates of specialization feel that even at this level teachers should not be required to teach all the subjects. They should be permitted to teach courses that they are most skilled and interested in. In this way students benefit from teacher enthusiasim as well as skill. Teachers should not be required to teach subjects in which they might be less able and interested.

I believe these arguments only encourage still more emphasis on the curriculum at the expense of individual students' needs. Specialization encourages maintenance of the lock step and forces depersonalization because of the masses of students that each teacher must cope with. Specialists in content subject areas are engaged in assembly-line-like instruction. The system works well with standardized machined parts that are identical and interchangeable, but it produces far too many casualties when it is imposed on children.

When it was discovered that there were unacceptably large numbers of students in each age group who could not compete, ability grouping and tracking procedures were developed. Even then, one level of instruction was provided for each group or track. Students were grouped in order to better fit the curricular offering. Alternative curricula were developed to fit the ability levels of students in the various tracks. Still more specialists were required for new curriculum content. There obviously remained many casualties in spite of our best grouping and tracking efforts.

These student casualties must need special consideration, so it was thought. Still more specialists emerged to identify their needs and then to provide for them. School psychologists appeared to identify, classify, and label these students with special needs. Reading specialists and special education teachers appeared to manage the problems of students who could not cope with the curricular requirements of any of the regular groups or tracks. These specialists emerged in response to needs produced by a system already dominated by specialists.

Specialists spawn more specialists. Specialists are accountable only for their specialty. If students are not benefiting from their special service, then the problem should be referred to another specialist. The referral process can become circular if no one of the specialists seems effective. New specialists emerge if enough students remain without finding a place with one of those already in existence. We create specialists to deal with problems that result from the specialist system.

The specialist system has had a considerable effect on teaching. This system approaches individual differences in learning ability primarily by tracking and grouping. Subject matter is organized for the specialist teacher. The specialist is concerned with the content of his or her subject or grade. They are isolated from other teachers and subject areas, and, consequently, they are unaware of the overall demands that the school and curriculum places on students. Specialists may develop unrealistic notions about the importance of the subject matter under their jurisdiction. Being specialists, they are unlikely to integrate other subject areas or skills teaching in their course work. If a student does not have some prerequisite skill for a specialist's subject, the teacher will be unlikely to note the fact or do anything to remedy it. The homework assignments will be the same for all of the students regardless of their range in ability. At the intermediate and secondary levels, the specialist teachers will see so many different students each day that they will not have time to devote to evaluating the problems that students have in doing their assignments. They will have scarcely enough time to check them and assign a grade.

The responsibility for learning shifts to the student. The specialist teacher is a dispenser of content. If students can't acquire the information being dispensed, that is not the specialist's fault. The grades awarded will simply reflect the extent to which the students have been able to benefit from the single instructional level.

Specialists must rely on ability grouping to help make sure that the students have the entry-level skills and ability to benefit from the instruction offered in their classrooms. If a great many students are doing poorly in a specialist's classroom, it will be because the students have been ill prepared or that this is just an extra-stupid group of students. It seldom occurs to the specialist to adjust instruction to the entry-level skills of the students entering his or her room. That would be an abhorrent thought to a specialist, the guardian of standards and curricular content.

Strict adherence to teaching specific curricular content has an extremely limiting effect on the way the specialist deals with individual differences in ability of students. Since the course content must be the same for all of the students in any given classroom, then the only elements that can be varied to fit are the modes or methods of presentation. The difficulty level of instruction, and consequently the entry-level skills of students, are not of concern. The entry-level skills of the students are supposed to be sufficient because of tracking and ability grouping. Variation in instructional method is intended to help students achieve up to the level of work provided in the class or grade.

Even when it is apparent that a student does not have the skill or ability to benefit from instruction in a particular grade or class, specialist teachers are unlikely to adjust the difficulty level of instruction. The extent to which this match is made is evidenced by scores and perform-ance levels on the work given each of the students. If the work is well matched, the scores and performance levels will be good. If the perform-ance is poor, it is most often the case that work given is not of the appropriate level; it is too hard.

Too often I have heard teachers predict which among students are likely to do well or fail as they move to advanced grades or classes. They are very accurate; it is tragic. Specialist teachers, with this foreknowledge of students' skill levels, willingly let them fail rather than adjust the curricular difficulty level to permit the students to succeed and achieve. Their curricular domain must remain inviolable.

Teacher training programs are guilty of preparing teachers to be specialists. The methods courses focus on content for particular levels and courses. The field experiences and practice teaching will also be at the specific site of the specialty. The training that teachers receive iso-lates them from other levels and areas of the curriculum. However, teachers will seldom, if ever, encounter a room full of students so well grouped that their achievement levels and instructional needs are as focused as the instruction the teachers are prepared to provide. When teachers aim their instruction, it is focused on their curricular slot. Their instruction will hit the target of those students who manage to fit the slot, but it will miss those students who are functioning either below or above it.

Specialist teachers are virtually helpless in the face of variability in achievement. Their instructional arsenal is aimed at a very narrow field. If students are failing grades or subjects, the primary strategy specialists have is to make the students repeat the course or grade. The specialist cannot aim at more than one target.

The arguments for specialization in teaching are superficially appealing. Teachers can concentrate on an area of their personal interest. They can maintain enthusiasm by teaching subjects or levels they like. They can teach only the subjects they are best at. There is an element of truth in these arguments. However, we must reform our perspective. We must concentrate our instructional effort and skills in delivering instruction to the diversity of students. We must break with the notion that we are teaching only a specific set of curricular objectives. Teachers really need to be quite familiar with many levels above and below their grade or course. We need to hold the success and achievement of individual students in greater esteem than we do the content of any curricular domain.

There inevitably comes a time when teachers need to be specialists. The training for careers and professions becomes increasingly technical. From medicine to auto mechanics, the skills and training become increasingly specialized. There are probably no longer in existence any mechanics who are sufficiently skilled to diagnose and repair all components of the modern car. Physicians must even specialize in the "general" practice of medicine. Our increasingly complex world requires specialization. There is a proliferation of curricular content and areas. We suffer from information overload. No one can be the general master of it all. There is not sufficient time or opportunity to even gain access to it all in one person's lifetime. However, for the K–12 curriculum, it is important for teachers to be generally informed about and competent to teach large sections of the curriculum. Teachers need to have the resources to teach students at whatever level they have attained when they walk into that teacher's room.

Teachers with special skills should serve as resources in collaborative arrangements with other teachers. Teachers with expertise in teaching and diagnosing problems in reading, writing, and math can assist other teachers in dealing with real problem students. Teachers with advanced expertise in any area should serve as resources for the academically talented students who are functioning well above the levels of the regular curricular offering.

Rather than concerning themselves with the broad range of needs of their students, the specialist may concentrate on the curricular subject. Curriculum specialists and textbook publishers concentrate and absorb more and more subject matter into each subject for the specialist teacher. It is obvious that the amount of information available to add to science and math curricula expands enormously moment by moment. National and international events in this densely populated world occur at an ever-expanding rate. The content of various areas of the social studies expands at the same rate. Students can be overwhelmed by such information and content loads. It is tempting for the specialist teacher to cram more in rather than to find out how much individual students can absorb and to consider then what is most relevant for individuals to learn.

Specialist teachers are the center of instruction. The students are there only to partake to the extent they are able. I advocate a complete change. Rather than content-centered teachers, we must have student-centered teachers. We need teachers who are specialists in producing continuous achievement progress in each student. Granted, the progress will cover a wide range, but there should be success and progress to the maximum extent possible for each student. The students must be the center of instruction and they must be engaged in learning. The teacher in this model is more of a manager, planner, and facilitator than the principle actor.

Teachers who are specialists have far too many students moving through their classrooms each day. It is extremely difficult to make instruction student centered in this way. Teachers should teach a broader range of subjects and thereby see many fewer students. The opportunity to integrate subject matter, particularly the language arts, is greater, and far more attention can be given to planning for individual needs. The time during the day can be used with greater flexibility and every student need not move in the same lock-step time frame.

Specialist teachers, lock-step curricula, and grades each interact and reinforce the continued existence of the others. Though some specialization is necessary and helpful, the specialist system as it is currently used and abused should be greatly modified.

Chapter 7

SCAPEGOATS

Grades permit blame for poor and failing performance to be assigned to the student. The students will bear the grade and also much of the blame if the grades are poor. Though the students are most often held responsible for the grades they receive, there are also other popular scapegoats.

We try to blame virtually everything but the system of grading itself and, of course, its two cohorts‡ the lock-step curriculum and the specialist. The process of finding scapegoats consumes much time in the ongoing rhetoric surrounding public education. There is profound irony in the process. Grading requires variability in performance. We must obtain a distribution of scores and grades; this is intrinsic in the system. However, when the poor grades in the distribution are assigned, as is inevitable, we look for a cause other than grading itself to explain why students do poorly. We avoid the notion that systems of grading themselves naturally result in poor performance as well as good.

Scapegoats permit us to avoid examining the actual source of the problem. Why we avoid looking at the real problem is a mystery. Why are grades held in such a sacrosanct position? Possibly a combination of convenience and tradition is the answer. Another reason we avoid being critical of grades may be that we have enough scapegoats to avoid dealing with the real problem.

The first grouping of scapegoats is made up of the students. Students are frequently blamed for their own poor grades and poor achievement. Poor grades are very often considered to be the result of laziness and lack of discipline. "If students would just work harder they could get better grades." "Students should pay better attention in class; they just don't seem to listen." "Some students are so busy misbehaving and acting up in class they can't learn anything."

Poor grades are often attributed to handicaps or disabilities in the students. There are literally dozens of labels for learning disabilities.

The most popular label is dyslexia. The term learning disability itself is now a generic label which includes dyslexia and the myriad other labels.

We often erroneously conclude that since most students do acceptably well in the educational system, all students should be capable of doing at least passing work. Consequently, if a student is not doing passing work, there must either be a defect in their character or their neurological makeup. We cannot accept the fact that the grading system itself is the culprit. We prefer to blame the students.

If the students are not selected as a scapegoat, then the students' parents may well be. There are a variety of reasons cited for the parents being at fault. "Parents are not concerned about how their children are doing in school." "There is no supervision at home. The kids just run wild." "Parents don't make their kids do their homework." "Both parents work all the time so they just don't have time or energy to make the kids keep up with their schoolwork." These comments are common among an even larger littany of complaints aimed at parents.

It is remarkable that we expect the parents of students who are doing poorly at school to make up for deficiencies in the school. If students can't do the work at school with the help of trained teachers, how can we expect the parents to do any better at home? It seems to me we have a double standard concerning parent involvement. The parents of poor-achieving students are responsible for their achievement while the teachers are responsible for that of the capable and gifted ones.

The social and cultural circumstances of the students and their families will be a target for blame if it is different than that of the normative group. Poverty and language differences are frequently singled out for blame.

The specialist system naturally lends itself to scapegoating. Each specialist teacher stakes out her or his curricular domain. Specialist teachers will not accept responsibility for any educational deficiency that is not a specific part of their domain. Blame for deficiencies in readiness or achievement, and the consequent failure of students in their classrooms, is readily passed on to previous teachers. When other teachers are blamed, they can readily shift the blame to child or his home.

There are other specialists in the system that can both point and be pointed to. Special education teachers, chapter I teachers, and school psychologists each have their assigned territory. Students that clearly don't fit the regular curricular domains will be referred to specialists such as these. They provide still more opportunities for fingerpointing in this system with an impressive array of potential scapegoats.

The hierarchy of administrators from principal to superintendent are also targetted for blame. The criticism includes things such as indifference, lack of support, discriminatory allocation of resources, and failure to uphold standards. Administrators are allusive targets. Some administrators seem to function as shields and deflectors of criticism. They become adept at redirecting criticism.

In such systems culpability is never settled. Fingers are pointed in every direction. Responsibility is continually shifted. The "buck" never stops.

The last two scapegoats are not specialists and they are not even human. Educational problems are often blamed on lack of standards and lack of resources. "If only we maintained high standards of achievement for all students, we wouldn't have such problems." We seem to feel that we could make lower-achieving students perform like high-achieving ones simply by demanding high standards of achievement. This usually leads to an unexpected double standard, challenge, hard work, and frustration for the lower-performing students, reasonable expectations and success for the higher-achieving ones.

We fail to recognize that high achievement requires a standard of reasonable and attainable objectives based on what students can do with optimum success and efficiency. High standards usually mean failure and frustration for the less able, and comfort and success for the able. What is needed are rationally determined standards for each individual student.

Lack of resources are a convenient, nonthreatening scapegoat. The lack of financial resources affects class size which is one of the most frequently blamed problems. The unavailability of special and supplementary texts and instructional materials is blamed as well. Currently, the supply and quality of the personal computer may be the culprit.

I should not claim that these scapegoats are devoid of culpability. There is an element of truth in all the claims and blames. There are in fact some slothful students who could do better with more effort. Some students could do better if they had some assistance at home. Certainly poverty affects achievement through health and nutrition, and children are particularly sensitive about the style and quality of their clothing. A few students will avoid school if they can't afford to dress the way they want to. So it is with all the areas mentioned as scapegoats; they do account for some problems, but they are small in number.

All six of these scapegoats are frequently cited because of the circular nature of scapegoating. Culpability is continually shifted so it is never settled. Virtually hidden from view in all this is the real culprit: grades.

Why does the culprit remain so well hidden? Grades are viewed as an effect, a symptom, rather than the cause or ailment itself. We believe that grades are simply passive signs of a problem. Our logic is faulty. We have confused cause with effect.

Such faulty logic is not without precedent in the contemplation of our educational difficulties. Consider the dropout problem. Two of the most common predictors of dropping out of school are poor reading achievement and having repeated grades—being held back one or more years. Both of these are viewed as causes of dropping out. In fact, however, only one of these is a cause. The other is only an effect of the underlying problem. Failing and repeating a grade is the result of lack of achievement. It may be the result of lack of reading achievement which is the other main antecedent of dropping out. Repeating grades is itself like dropping out. It is the consequence of failure and poor achievement. The problem with repeating grades is one of not providing instruction at an appropriate difficulty level for students so they can make continuous progress at whatever their individual learning rate is.

Because we confuse cause with effect, we often assume that by stopping the practice of making students repeat grades we will reduce the ultimate dropout rate. We avoid looking at the real problem that causes the retention and that will ultimately cause the students to drop out. The real effective practice needed for use with the students at risk for dropping out is to provide for a good match of instructional difficulty which in turn permits continuous achievement progress for them (Slavin & Madden, 1989; Hargis, 1989).

Grades are very much responsible for contradicting the use of continuous progress approaches to instruction. Continuous achievement requires continuous success. Success and achievement are marked by acceptable and better grades. We are required, however, to give a wide distribution of grades. This precludes using continuous progress approaches. The lock-step curriculum is the antithesis of individualized, continuous progress approaches. Moreover, the lock-step organization is necessary to give a wide distribution of grades.

Success is a requirement of continuous progress approaches. Every one of the individuals who were listed as scapegoats are responsible for insuring the ongoing success of all students. Everyone should share the responsibility for seeing that every student is continuously working at an instructional level that produces the success that is the necessary evidence that achievement is occurring.

Specialists teachers are isolated in their classrooms and protected from accountability by grades. Their grade books provide evidence of the variable performance of the students that pass through their rooms. The testing and grading of assignments is conducted solely to record in such a manner. Performance is supposed to be variable so poor performance can be assigned the poor grades. The contradiction is overlooked, and teachers are not held accountable for insuring that each student is working at an instructional level that permits success and achievement. If questioned about why students are failing in their classes, the specialist teacher can go through the littany of scapegoats and find one or more that will justify the grades.

Smaller classes is a commonly cited factor in poor achievement. However, smaller classes will make no difference in achievement if one level of instruction is still provided. A distribution of grades will still result, and the students who are working at the frustration end of the distribution will still show poor achievement.

Students cannot be working at their individual instructional levels, making continuous progress, and be graded at the same time. Here is where the conflict with grading occurs. When all the performance is good, then all the grades should be good. Grades lose all meaning, as they should if a continuous progress model of instruction is adopted.

The number of different students that specialist teachers deal with each day is a problem. This is not the same thing as large class size, however. Specialist teachers at the secondary level may encounter more than 150 different students each day. This reduces a teacher to a grading automaton. It isolates teachers from each other and it places their students in isolated competitive relationships with each other. This condition further limits the possibility of introducing a continuous progress model of instruction. The only way that classrooms can be organized to produce continuous progress is through cooperation. Students need to help each other. Peer tutoring and cooperative learning teams are necessary.

Specialists scapegoat. Scapegoating is evidence of the isolation of each specialist. If there was really no one to blame, if continuous progress became the goal for every student, each professional who has a role to play in helping students learn could work helpfully and cooperatively.

Chapter 8

SUCCESS, FAILURE, AND ACHIEVEMENT

"Nothing succeeds like success" is an adage that is widely accepted. However, the educational establishment qualifies their acceptance of this old truism. The system admonishes students to succeed, to be "winners," but it makes the students entirely responsible for the attainment of success. We should take the old adage completely to heart. Success is the fundamental ingredient in achievement. We should make capital of this fact. Success should be the responsibility of the educational system. It should be the principle guiding instructional delivery.

The importance of success can be explained in very simple terms with very simple examples. To learn any skill, one must perform it in practice with sufficient repetition to acquire it with permanency. In learning a sight word, a spelling word, or a math fact, students must associate the correct response with each item enough times in practice to learn the correct answer. If the correct answer is not linked with the stimulus item enough times, the item will remain unknown or, perhaps worse, an incorrect answer will be learned in its place. When students make consistent mistakes on seatwork and assignments, they are at risk for learning the wrong answer. Remember, if one is getting the right answer, then one is learning the right answer. However, the reverse is also true.

Getting the wrong answer can lead to learning that answer. In math activities, especially drill activities, there is much opportunity to learn wrong answers. In this way error patterns are acquired. Error patterns are of considerable concern. They cause more problems than not knowing an answer at all. There is so much practicing of errors that Ashlock's (1986) book on error patterns in math is in its fourth expanded edition.

Students who experience extended periods of failure have abundant opportunity to learn wrong answers. For this reason many of these students require remedial instruction. Remedial instruction is required to break down error patterns and then learn the correct answers. Remedial instruction is very time consuming and inefficient. The problem behaviors a student has learned must be identified, unlearned, and replaced by the appropriate response or strategy. Just identifying the many different problems can be very difficult. It is far better to provide success experiences in the first place so that correct answers are learned.

Learning activities must be set up so that students will arrive at the correct answer. Performance on activities must ultimately be close to error free to avoid learning incorrect answers. The high scores and performance of the ablest learners should provide the standard to be used for all students. Carefully constructing the learning activities that help students arrive at the correct responses is the most fundamentally important component of good instruction.

Grades work against good instruction. Grades require errors. Grades require a range of performance in a classroom in order to provide a comparable range in grades. One level of instruction lends itself quite nicely to producing a wide range of performance. This, however, will be poor instruction no matter how its delivery is ornamented or embellished. It permits some students to do poorly and to fail. It produces students who will require remedial instruction and students who are at risk for dropping out.

How should instructional activities be prepared to produce success? How is adequate success for optimal learning determined? Actually, much of this information has long been available. In reading and reading-related activities, Emmett Betts (1946) provided excellent guidelines. In order to determine if students were reading in material of appropriate difficulty, he devised a system of observation to be used while students were reading.

Betts provided standards of difficulty for matching reading material with individual students. These are standards used to make sure that students can successfully read in the instructional materials being provided. Briefly stated, the guidelines are these: For reading instruction, a student should encounter unknown words in a range of 2 to 4 percent and have at least 75 percent comprehension. This level of difficulty is called the instructional reading level. If the instructional reading material meets these guidelines with a student, then that material is appropriate for use in teaching reading to that student. The next level that Betts described is the independent or basal level. Here, the student should encounter fewer than 2 percent unknown words, and the student's comprehension level should be at least 90 percent. Reading material at this level could be used with no teacher assistance. The student could use it independently. It was also the level at which the student could read recreationally and learn to enjoy reading.

Betts described a third reading level, which is to be avoided. This is the frustration reading level. It occurs when students encounter more than about 4 percent unknown words. At this point, the reading becomes labored and stressful, and comprehension falls off abruptly. The percentage of new words may sound small, but it means that the reader will encounter a new word in twenty running words, or about a new word in every other sentence. The context is disrupted, comprehension cannot be maintained and the reader feels frustrated.

Students' reading behavior is observed while reading orally to determine the load of unknown words, and comprehension is checked by asking them a set of questions directed to the passage just read. Betts recommended that the difficulty level of the reading material be adjusted to produce the desired reading behavior in the students.

It is ironic that the reading behavior of students is not often used as the basis for adjusting the difficulty level of the reading instructional material they are using. It is used as the basis for giving grades. If a student happens to be lucky enough to be one for whom the reading material in use happens to be at the independent reading level, then that student will get an "A". If the student is among the group for whom the material is at the instructional reading level, then that student will get a "C" or "B". Finally, if the reading material is at a frustration level for the student, he or she will get poor or failing grades. Reading behavior is seldom used to insure success; it is used to give grades.

In schoolwork that does not always include reading, such as spelling and math drill and seatwork activities, instructional levels are determined by the percentage correct. Since learning occurs when a student practices getting things correct, the percentage correct should necessarily be high. Good practice work means a high percentage correct. Ninety percent accuracy or correct answers is indicative of good practice. Here there is little opportunity to practice errors. Gickling and Thompson (1985) suggest that 70 to 80 percent accuracy on drill and seatwork activities is a range that indicates an instructional level. Again, we do not usually use performance on routine work activities as a device for adjusting the difficulty level of the activity to produce the desired performance levels. We simply use the performance to assign grades.

Notice that good performance, 90 percent plus, is that level usually given the top grades. Instructional-level performance is awarded good to average grades. Remember, however, that these guidelines are the same for all students. Instruction should continually be adjusted to produce the same appropriate scores for all students. Using the scores to assign grades is a terrible negative practice.

The instructional level in reading or any other schoolwork activity has important implications for success. This is the fact that work of appropriate difficulty permits students to be engaged in learning.

Academically engaged time (Rosenshine & Berliner, 1978) or academic learning time (Gickling & Thompson, 1985) is an essential ingredient in learning. Simply put, the more time you can spend in a learning activity, the more you will learn. Activities that are at an instructional level of difficulty permit a student to stay engaged in learning. Instructional activities that exceed the difficulty levels outlined above are not actually instructional at all. They are frustratingly difficult. It is comprised of work that is too difficult to do, is confusing, and creates stress in the student. Students cannot long remain engaged in activities they can't do, and certainly they cannot really be engaged in learning if they are unable to do the thing. The opportunity to practice errors is great. Students may develop inefficient, random approaches to doing their work. Some students learn to give up helplessly when encountering any academic activity (Grimes, 1981).

Students do not willingly and voluntarily fail. It is the work set before them that causes them to do so. If it is structured to their individual instructional levels, it will permit them to succeed. Scoring of schoolwork should not be done to flag failing students. It should be done to determine if it is within instructional-level limits so that the benefits of success can be achieved. Remember, the scores required to indicate success are the same for all students. Score are the evidence of the quality of the match between students and their work. Scores should be kept in the success range to maximize time engaged in learning and to increase the students' learning efficiency.

When students are able to engage effectively in an activity, they will get better and better at it. This is the essence of the adage, "Nothing succeeds like success." This holds true in whatever one is attempting to learn. Granted, there are limits to the amount of improvement possible in most activities. Our limits are determined by our physical endowments and our talent. Still, the adage is true whether it concerns learning to read, to play golf, to play a musical instrument, or to be a mechanic. The opposite is also true. If you engage in an activity ineffectively or poorly, you will likely not improve and may well get worse. These phenomena make up what are called Matthew effects (Stanovich, 1986; Hargis et al., 1988; Hargis, 1989). Matthew effects explain the "rich-get-richer-and-the-poor-get-poorer" phenomenon.

Matthew effects are a concept that comes from the Gospel according to Saint Matthew.

> For whosoever hath, to him shall be given, and he shall have more abundance: but whosoever hath not, from him shall be taken away even that he hath. (XIII:12)
>
> For unto everyone that hath shall be given, and he shall have abundance: but from him that hath not shall be taken away even that which he hath. (XXV:29)

Stanovich (1986) described Matthew effects in learning to read. For example, as students acquire reading skill, opportunities for reading open all around them. Printed information is everywhere. Reading is needed in all other subject areas as well. A wealth of reading opportunities occurs to students who are succeeding in learning to read. Practice opportunities for reading will continually increase.

The students who fail, however, seems to make no progress. They appear to do worse as time goes by. They cannot benefit from all the incidental opportunities for reading practice that surround them. They are not able to use reading in other subject areas. They cannot read for pleasure. They fall farther and farther behind their higher-achieving peers and farther and farther behind their own potential. They feel increasingly frustrated, helpless, and ineffective. Each of these feelings further compounds their problem.

Unfortunately, failure is an institution in our educational system. We expect failure because it is part of our grading system. Also, failure is our primary diagnostic tool. Students must fail and fail abjectly before anything is done for them. Then, what is done ignores their primary problem which is failure.

The link between success and achievement is a direct one. Programs that capitalize on success are scarce, however. Slavin (1989) evaluated and catalogued effective programs that have success as a central focus. He places these systems in a category that are operated under what he calls continuous progress models. The student's individual readiness or entry-level skills are assessed. Each student proceeds at her or his own pace. Frequent measurements are taken to insure that each student is succeeding and making satisfactory progress. Adjustments in instructional difficulty level are constantly made so that success is continuous.

Programs that use curriculum-based assessment of necessity focus on success (Hargis, 1987, 1989). This measurement technique is designed to make sure that instructional activity and materials are matched to students in order to produce success.

Cooperative learning systems and peer tutoring programs typically protect students from failure and provide peer support to help students be successful at each learning step. Students are supposed to do well in these systems. Fellow students are to help one another get their work done correctly.

Grades are an obstacle to the implementation of these systems. Success and continuous progress for all are antithetic to our grading system. Our grading system requires that some students do poorly.

Measurement for grades takes the focus of assessment from its more important function as a tool for learning. Measurement should be used to determine if a student is engaged in the right level of instructional activity. Errors on work are not something merely to be tallied. They are to be used to provide corrective feedback. Errors uncorrected are errors practiced.

The question arises: "If students are supposed to get everything right, where is the challenge?" The answer to this question requires that a distinction be made between work and busywork. In routine schoolwork, new items on the curriculum are continually being introduced. These new items may need practice to process them from short-term to more permanent memory storage. As has been emphasized, this work must be done successfully. Busywork, on the other hand, is simply giving students work that they have already committed to permanent storage. It is already mastered. Work like this is given just to occupy time. It is a useless activity.

Doing appropriate work, even though accuracy and scores are high, is challenging. The challenge, however, should never exceed the student's ability to get good instructional-level scores and to be able to stay engaged in learning.

The lower-achieving students are challenged far too much. They should be challenged at the same level as their higher-achieving peers. The work and achievement will be proceeding at different rates, but the maximum benefits to each student occur only when her or his performance is high. The performance scores should be in the same range for both high- and low-achieving students. The performance scores should be the same even though the amount of curricular progress is different.

When the scores are the same for both high- and low-achieving students, Matthew effects will benefit the low achievers also. Certainly there will be differences in achievement, but the achievement will be a maximum.

Keeping students supplied with work at appropriate instructional levels means that the student will spend their time engaged in learning. Students can't for very long remain engaged in tasks that are too difficult for them. If the tasks are too difficult, what looks like engaged time probably will be nothing more than the students' staring at the work in puzzlement. This activity can't last for long. Other times the students will simply be doing the work incorrectly. When students aren't engaged in learning, they will be engaged in something else. Frustration-level work produces a variety of off-task behaviors. Some of these may not be disruptive, like quiet daydreaming, but in other students it may be disruptive. Teacher time is much better spent in preparing instructional-level activities for all students than in trying to cope with annoying and disruptive off-task behavior.

Success and achievement are essential for the self-concept of students. Failure is damaging and must be avoided. Chronic failure often produces severe emotional and behavior problems in students, and it is certainly responsible for the majority of dropouts.

Students that are constantly given frustration-level work to do have little prospect for getting passing grades without cheating. Failure does produce cheating in many of these students out of simple desperation. Actually, the competitive nature of grading causes cheating in students at all achievement levels. Fear of a lower grade can be as demoralizing to the higher-achieving students as failure is to the lower achievers.

Chapter 9

GRADES AS ETIOLOGY

Grades, like microbes, cause many problems. As has been stated many times before in this essay, however, grades are seldom thought of as a cause. They are usually viewed as simply a symptom. This is an erroneous idea. Grades are not symptoms of problems. The institution of grading and the educational structures that require grading are the active agents in the cause of many of our educational ills.

Why has the cause and effect link been overlooked? The answer may be that there are a number of intermediate stages in grade-induced illnesses. In this chapter, I will attempt to describe the various ills and list the stages in their development.

Learning disabilities, of all the educational ills that may befall students, is usually considered the most like a physical disease. It is usually thought of as having an organic basis, a neurological dysfunction. However, it may be argued that most cases of learning disabilities are caused by grades (Hargis & Terharr-Yonkers, 1989).

The malady of another group of students who also are ultimately referred to special education is classed as behavior disorders. Students with the more severe forms of this condition are often classed as emotionally disturbed. A substantial portion of this population of students owe their behavioral disabilities to grading.

Prominent among our list of educational ills is the dropout problem. I believe that fully 80 percent of the students that drop out, or are pushed out, of school have failing grades as the origin of the difficulties.

Cheating on homework, tests, and papers is a common problem. Cheating is attributable to the competitive environment created by the grading system. Competition exists at all ability levels. Some students are attempting to avoid failure, and some are struggling to maintain the top grades.

The social nature of humans is countered by the competitive isolation that grades cause. This isolated, competitive environment is far different from the social interactive environment where learning normally takes place outside of school. The grading system contributes to the alienation and social isolation of students, and it does nothing to encourage the development of social skills needed to learn and work in the real world. What would be considered normal helpful interactive behavior outside of school would be considered cheating in school.

Grading dictates the form of much instructional activity in schools. Each grade-controlled step in the instructional routine will produce some reaction in students. The behavioral consequence of this reaction will be either adaptive or maladaptive within the structure of the school. A single instructional level is used to induce the required range of grades. This condition sets in motion the sequence of events to which students will be compelled to react.

The lower-achieving students in the typical classroom will have the most difficulty coping with the single level of instruction. They will ultimately be the recipients of the "F's" and "D's". In the process of serving their function of doing poorly and filling out the low portion of the grade distribution, they will encounter work in which they cannot effectively engage. The work will typically be at a frustration level if they are to get the failing grades. Work of this difficulty level, by definition, is frustrating and largely incomprehensible. Students cannot long remain engaged in tasks that they simply can't do.

Many students with so-called attention deficit disorders are simply suffering from frustration-level work, work to which it is not possible to attend for any length of time, let alone engage in. Their off-task, distracted behavior is symptomatic of the frustration-level work, not a symptom of an organically based disability. Much distractible, even hyperdistractible, behavior can be directly attributed to the difficulty level of the task a student is required to do when the behavior is occurring (Thompson, V. P., Gickling, E. E., and Havertape, J. F., 1983). Control the task difficulty, and much behavior is effectively controlled.

Attention and distraction problems are often associated with learning disabled students. They are related to task difficulty. So are other off-task behaviors. If a student is unable to remain engaged in a task, then that student will be engaged in some off-task activity. If the behavior is disruptive, then the student is at risk for being identified as behavior disordered. Students who seldom have opportunity to engage in instructional-level activity will have lots of off-task time. The students whose off-task time is quiet and unannoying will usually be left alone. However, the students whose off-task time is annoying will be a burden and their teachers will be far more interested in getting them labeled and purged from their classrooms.

Off-task behavior can be more than merely annoying. Students that have endured chronic stress and frustration without the hope of improving their lot may act out in aggressive and very disruptive ways. A student's reaction to failure depends on an enormous variety of personality and background variables. Some students simply avoid and withdraw from the source of their frustration. A variety of in-school avoidance strategies emerge such as cutting classes and truancy. These behaviors exacerbate the students' difficulties, but they are preferred by teachers to the students who strike out aggressively against the source of their misery, the school.

The more disruptive students labeled as behavior disordered or emotionally disturbed can then be moved to special education programs. The truant students may find themselves in serious trouble if their behavior leads to the legal system. Truant students usually drop out when they reach a legal age. However, they can become status offenders and so find themselves caught in the correctional system, their problems compounded tenfold.

There is an intermediate group of students, those whose behavior is not worthy of special education referral but whose behavior is significantly annoying. The system deals with these students by suspension and expulsion. These students are the pushouts. There is irony in the fact that attendance problems are often handled by suspension, truancy by expulsion.

Students at the low end of the achievement continuum find themselves in hopeless situations in regard to alleviating the frustration of failure and attaining the emotional relief of reasonable success and achievement. The competitive environment created by the grading system isolates them from their natural social inclination to seek help and help others with the tasks before them. What should be a natural productive activity is viewed as unethical and immoral. Given no way of seeking relief from failure and damage to self-concept, students inevitably cheat. Cheating is directly attributable to the grading system.

Cooperative learning systems have demonstrated effectiveness. These systems require helpful social interaction. In competitive classrooms much of the activity that is necessary to the function of cooperative learning is considered as cheating.

Cooperative social skills are necessary to leading effective lives outside of school. Competitive classrooms do not foster the development of important social skills. Instead of developing and encouraging social skill development, we find that children are alienated from each other. Grades contribute to unhealthy, unkind, and competitive relationships. The least able are the most damaged by the system.

I have argued that the majority of our educational problems are self-inflicted and to a great extent due to grades and grading-related practices. Nevertheless, there are students whose problems do not stem from grades. Their problems originate within themselves or in the environment outside of school. Despite the fact that both groups exhibit the same behaviors, it matters where the problem resides. How do we separate the two groups of students? How do we differentiate the educational treatment of the two? Since the behavior of the two groups is the same, should not their treatment be the same?

In order to separate "real" learning and behavior disordered children from the much larger group of curriculum casualties, we must determine whether their particular problem behavior is the result of, or the cause of, failure. To do this it is necessary to provide instructional activities and materials that are clearly within students' ability level. Then while the students are engaging in the activities their behavior is observed.

If the material and activities provided to the student are matched with their individual instructional levels, he or she should be able to engage in doing them. Behavior should demonstrate this engagement. The observation may have to continue over several days while maintaining this instructional level. Some students who have experienced chronic frustration and failure with virtually all instructional activities have learned to react to it in a stereotyped pattern. Most usually, however, when students are given material that they can do, they will engage in it rather readily. If there remains residual off-task behavior after the students have had a reasonable opportunity to be engaged, then the learning problem is due to causes other than in the difficulty level of the materials. In these cases the off-task behavior itself or its other cause will have to be dealt with directly. Students so identified are not curriculum casualties. They are the "real" learning disabled.

It is necessary to separate real learning disabled students from curriculum casualties so that appropriate instructional decisions can be made. In every case it is necessary to provide for the instructional-level needs of individual students, but it is also necessary to determine if there is a cause outside the grading system and curriculum mismatch. Appropriate instructional-level material is an essential, but occasionally insufficient ingredient for producing sufficient on-task behavior in "real" learning disabled and behavior disordered students. The assessment procedure is automatic if the students' instructional level needs are being met. If this is being done, residual off-task behavior suggests further attention is necessary. In some students, the behavior itself must be the focus of special intervention.

If a student's attention span does not extend to the time of normally assigned work periods, twenty to fifty minutes, the work should be shortened so that the task is within his or her attention limitation. The student needs to experience the success of task completion. After the student has had consistent success with task completion, the work periods may be extended.

The attention problems of some students may result from extra sensitivity to distraction. This sensitivity should be managed initially by changing the instructional environment to reduce distraction to within the student's tolerance threshold. Study carrels, quiet areas, or soundproofing may be needed to provide an environment that permits task completion. After the student has had consistent opportunity to work within his or her distraction threshold, the student's tolerance threshold should be gradually extended to more normal levels.

In other cases the cause of a student's problems may result from things that can't be managed by adjusting the curriculum or instructional environment. For example, a student who is chronically hungry is not likely to attend well even under optimal instructional conditions. Here, the most appropriate intervention has to be something to eat. Lack of sleep, allergies, and other chronic health problems will also need a noncurricular intervention.

In most cases grades and grade-related practices are the root cause of learning problems. However, some students' learning problems may to some extent be within themselves or may exist somewhere in the out-of-school environment. Nevertheless, regardless of where the cause lies, the first approach with them should always be in identifying and providing instructional-level teaching. Doing this is not only necessary for adequate achievement to begin, but it is also the necessary basis for the next level of assessment. This is the observation of behavior at the instructional level. Can the student remain on task and engaged in learning during instructional-level activities is the question this observation is to answer. Any remaining off-task behavior suggests that the behavior itself will need special education, or that there is a cause outside the educational system.

Chapter 10

GRADING THE ACADEMICALLY TALENTED

Academically talented students, by definition, are supposed to do well in school. Their accomplishments in school usually define them. The accomplishments may be demonstrated in high achievement test scores and/or grades. There are some academically talented students that do not demonstrate their academic potential in the classroom, however.

Grades make it possible for some of these students to go unnoticed. For example, no attention will be directed to a student with high achievement potential, if that student is doing average work compared to his or her age peers. Students like this will simply blend in. When one instructional level from the curriculum is provided in a classroom, there will be no opportunity for some students to achieve beyond that level provided. If the students are not particulary motivated by grades and competition, they may be quite satisfied to coast along with average to good grades and take life easy.

The fact is that the range of achievement in every grade includes performance that is much higher than the grade designation. How is it that some students demonstrate achievement years in advance of their grade placement? We know that in the lock-step curriculum only grade-level curricular items are presented. How is it that some students acquire academic skills far in advance of those being presented in their classrooms?

The students that achieve at higher levels than their grade placement are obviously engaged in learning activities in addition to those in the classroom. Some learn incidentally or directly from older siblings. They may learn from exposure or direct assistance from parents. Some are highly motivated by interest and pursue academic subjects quite independently. Quick learning rates and the enjoyment of reading will expand reading skill rapidly as these students engage in much extra incidental and recreational reading. The positive side of the Matthew effects are very apparent with these students.

The high achievement and classroom performance demonstrated by these students is likely made possible by a reasonable threshold of advantage in their home life. This advantage is not available to all students who have high achievement potential. Availing themselves of the grade level of instruction only will not advance these students much, if any, beyond it. Academic potential and talent cannot transcend lack of opportunity. Getting adequate grades in an age-appropriate grade will hide the achievement potential of these able students. The grading system permits this to occur. In fact, these underachieving students are actually conforming to the lock-step organization.

Some academically talented students are unwittingly punished for their high achievement. The problem for them is the mirror image of what happens to students who are given frustration-level work to do. Work that is too hard produces off-task behavior, but sometimes so does work that is too easy. Some academically talented students have a very low tolerance level for work that is too easy for them. It is simply viewed as busywork. Many students conform, do the work, and occupy their time with their own mental resources. Some, though, will be off task in annoying ways. In the more extreme cases, the students get into serious confrontations with the system.

Grades can mask the fact that students are not working at their individual instructional level. When one level of instruction is used, the higher-achieving students will inevitably get high scores and grades while performing in it. The work may be well below their own instructional level, but since the scores and grades are high, everyone assumes that everything is fine. The students, particulary the younger ones, will be unaware that they could be performing at a higher level. School is very easy and these students may be a little bored, but they can manage to find things to engage themselves in to get through each day. School is not nearly as unpleasant a place for them as it is for the students at the low end of the achievement continuum who find themselves with work which is above their individual instructional level.

Some schools have policies to deal with the academically able that conform to lock-step policies. I am aware of schools that permit more able students to do work one grade level above their actual grade placement. This was a policy that was rigorously enforced, in spite of the evidence from the assessment records of their students that showed achievement considerably in advance of this. This school happened to be serving an affluent community, and the mean reading achievement of each grade level was a full standard deviation above the norms on the standardized achievement test they used. A great many of the students in every classroom were actually achieving at levels several grades above the additional one allowed.

Grades cannot be a meaningful index of the performance of academically talented students. They can only indicate in a general way in which portion of the achievement curve a student is. They give no specific information as to level of achievement or to the specifics of what the students are actually capable of learning.

For the students who are bored and demonstrating annoying off-task behaviors, teachers may give grades that include measures of motivation and interest. For example, a teacher may comment, "He shows no interest, I'll give him a C." These factors, however, have nothing directly to do with actual achievement. These are more a reflection of the quality of the match between the classroom's instructional level and that of the student. Students appear unmotivated and uninterested if the schoolwork they are required to do is for them simply busywork.

Many of us have a strong need to control the students and make them conform to the curricular standard. All students must do the work required in that classroom. This attitude dominates over the actual instructional needs of individual students. The more creative and independent of these students may chafe at these controls and be in constant conflict with their teachers.

For academically talented students who are identified as such and have access to special programs, grading can pose a variety of new pitfalls. Only one approach, acceleration, will permit students who are being moved ahead of their age peers to work at a pace where grades do not pose a problem. Students being accelerated will be working with a peer group of similar achievers. If a student has been moved up to the point where performance is within the instructional level provided in that class or grade, then good grades will be forthcoming and no problems with grading will be experienced.

Other systems of dealing with academically talented students are potentially troublesome if traditional grading methods are used. I am referring to those programs that segregate these students either full or part time. Some school systems may have full-time special classes or schools for the academically talented. Others may provide advanced classes or honors classes for them. If these programs place these students in competition for grades, they may have negative consequences. The competition often is inordinately great. If the teachers of such programs feel they must award a distribution of grades, students that would routinely get high grades in regular class placement now will receive average or below grades. The competition for high grades will be demoralizing for many students. They will want to avoid such programs. Why jeopardize your grade point average and be hassled in a stressful competitive situation? It is better to stay in the regular classes even if they are kind of boring.

In such competitive programs too much attention is diverted from learning to getting a high grade. Students attend to what the teachers' idiosyncracies are in the way they grade, what kinds of tests they prepare, and how to please or ingratiate themselves with the teachers. Such programs are not healthy learning environments.

The use of grades in programs for the academically talented is rationalized in some very questionable ways. Some claim that these students should experience the same competition that their more average peers do. Also, the talented students need to experience failure and disappointment the same as other students.

When academically talented students remain in regular classrooms, grades can have a squelching effect on their achievement. High grades leave the impression that the students are doing very well. They are given their performance relative to others on the single level of instruction. Since students are conditioned to work for grades and they do not focus on learning, there will be no reason for them to advance in their study beyond the point required to get the top grades. The performance required to get the top grades in the lock-step classroom often is far below the achievement potential of these students. The students, having this misplaced purpose for their studies, feel that their objective has been attained, and the idea that they should pursue studies in the subject further does not occur to them. Even if it did occur to them, the opportunity for the further pursuit of a topic would be limited.

Ideally, students should be permitted to move through subjects and grade levels at their individual learning rate without regard to lock-step order. The students could work at the most advanced level of their capability at which they could still get high scores and grades. However, this approach to the education of the academically talented is the most controversial.

There are a variety of reasons given in criticism of acceleration. Some feel that students should be kept with their chronological age peers regardless of what their peer group might be in terms of academic achievement. They feel that the students need to conform to the curriculum standards. Some feel that there is a standard period for emotional and social development, and so all students should remain with their age peers. This all in spite of evidence that most academically talented students are generally advanced in these social areas as well.

Many of the problems that confront accelerated students are problems of accelerating through conventional lock-step organization. If the schools had more flexibility in organization as well as in grading, many of these problems would disappear. There are organizational systems that permit and even encourage students to work at an individually appropriate pace. Multigraded classrooms have always permitted and even encouraged this. Nongraded plans attempted to encourage this. Student-centered systems of instructional delivery are very conducive to individual pacing. Supervised study systems, peer tutoring, and cooperative learning approaches all encourage rates of learning that can be considerably in advance of the chronological age average. The continuous progress model described by Slavin (1989) promotes accelerated learning. Curriculum-based assessment (Hargis, 1987) is an educational measurement technique that requires that students be working at whatever level matches their current achievement stage.

Acceleration is really a misnomer when we are speaking of the academically talented. We can really make no one achieve faster than their individual capabilities. What we really are doing is permitting students to work at a pace which is individually comfortable and appropriate for them. When we make these students march through school in the lock step we artificially retard their progress.

In any of the approaches that are conducive to accelerated learning, conventional grading does not function well.

Grades mask what the real rate of achievement might be for individual students. All the students receiving an "A" grade in a classroom are not actually performing at their best instructional level. This might be so for some students but not for others. This single grade does not reveal the wide range of achievement levels that exist among those students who receive it. Some students in every classroom are capable of making the same grade at achievement levels that far exceed their current grade placement. These students should be permitted to work at the highest level they are inclined to at which they can still receive a high grade. That is, if grades need be given at all.

Chapter 11

GRADE-INDUCED ASSESSMENT PROBLEMS

Grades appear to exist simply as a result of assessment activity. However, grades are really the dominating factor in the nature of educational assessment itself.

Grades themselves, unfortunately, are an important assessment device. They are the measure used to make major decisions in the lives of children. Passing grades are, by definition, necessary for the rites of passage that society has assigned largely to the schools; passing grades are necessary to make the transitions between elementary, middle or junior high, and high school as well as the grade levels that move through all of them. Failing grades, on the other hand, are our primary diagnostic tool. Not only can grades impede and disrupt the rights of passage, they may change the course of a child's life. They can lead to two diagnoses and two ultimate labels. One of the labels says handicapped and the other says dropout.

Students who are most out of synchronization with the curriculum may do failing work in almost all subjects. Most students who will get the label of mild retardation are identified this way. First, failing to pass the primary grade curriculum, these students will be referred for further evaluation. Evaluation with intelligence tests and measures of adaptive behavior will confirm that many of these students fit this category. But the first stage in the diagnostic process is getting failing grades.

Failing grades is the first diagnostic step in the identification of learning disabled students. Students who are referred for further evaluation, but intelligence testing shows IQ's in the normal range, will get still more evaluation. There are a many tests that measure cognitive and perceptual deficits that can qualify students for the label learning disabled. Students may qualify for the LD label in this way, but still the first step is failing grades.

For many unfortunate students who will ultimately receive the LD label, the process is painfully drawn out. They must fail and receive failing grades for a very long time in order to get the label. No obvious evidence other than continued failing grades can be found to indicate a learning disability. Consequently, no special help will likely be available for them. The academic ability level of the students is sufficiently below that required for adequate performance in their age-grade placement. They are unable to progress even at a modest rate. Still, it may take several years of failure before a discrepancy between their achievement level and their potential for achievement reaches the dimension required to qualify as learning disabled. These are the students that I have called curriculum casualties. This is a label that more accurately fits the problem. It assumes the source of their problem is not in the student but in the lock-step curriculum.

The students who ultimately drop out invariably receive failing grades as well. There has been enough failure that they will have been retained in one or two grades. These students have managed to make sufficient progress that a significant discrepancy does not emerge between their potential for achievement and their actual achievement. They are unlikely to receive help because they qualify for no label. Nevertheless, their academic skill never reaches the level needed to do passing work in many of their classes. So, without prospects for doing better or for graduation, these students drop out. This pattern of failure and failing grades identifies over 80 percent of the students who will ultimately drop out (Kronick & Hargis, 1989).

It may be true that many mildly retarded and some learning disabled students should be in special classes, but why do they have to go through failure to get there? It seems heartless to permit failure to go on and on as is the case with these students. The tradition of grading is too strong. All of the measurement effort that could be going into identifying the instructional needs of students instead goes into finding out what their grades are. We feel we must give grades so we must test to find out what grades to give. We seem helpless to do otherwise.

Having grades compels us to test in order to find out what grades go with each student. Having grades compels us to give one level of instruction and provide one level of material. Only in this way will our assessment show the distribution of grades that we must produce. Assessment becomes a passive instrument used to label students with grades. It should be an active procedure for altering the instruction to match the students with appropriate instructional activity and material so that all students will do well.

Grades require us to measure a student's performance on a particular task, and then the student is graded for it. We should be required to do the virtual reverse of this. We should measure the difficulty of tasks given the performance of particular students and then the tasks graded in regard to each student. The objective of assessment should be grading tasks instead of students in order to adjust the task difficulty to fit the students' individual needs.

Assessment is a static process because of grades. The students are graded on fixed sets of curricular material assigned to their grades or classes. The students are variable in ability, so their performance and the grades produced while working in the fixed curriculum will be variable. The curriculum and the student performance in it comprises the main part of assessment. In order to produce grades the curriculum must be the same for the students in each class or grade. In effect then, the test must be the same difficulty for all students in order to produce the desired range of grades.

Assessment and instruction should be a far more dynamic process. All students should be experiencing success in their instructional endeavors, and the only way this is possible is to change the curricular offering to match the individual skill level of each student. This means that assessment procedures must change to a matching process. Since the curriculum and student performance in it forms the basis of assessment, this means that the curriculum must be in a dynamic and fluid state to keep student performance at the level indicating optimum success and achievement. In other words, the tests are constantly being changed in order to produce the same scores. Grading contradicts this process.

Grades cause assessment to be separated from instruction. However, assessment should be an integral part of instruction. Teachers avoid testing unless and until they must determine a grade to enter in the grade book or put on the report card. Testing for grades has virtually nothing to do with instruction. Testing should be integrated with teaching in order to match instructional activity to students and to provide helpful feedback. It should be a regular and direct part of all instrucion.

Assessment for grades is something to fear for many students. Test anxiety surely stems from the grading and labeling function of most testing that currently goes on. Students should not feel fear and apprehension about assessment. It should be done primarily for adjusting instruction and providing feedback. There should be no grading or labeling consequences. It should be a constant part of all instructional activity and should come to be viewed as a normal part of instruction itself. Assessment should provide support and assistance to students. If students think about assessment at all, it should be with this positive view.

If assessment were used appropriately as a part of instruction, grade books would have to change into a record of what the students were doing and what they had mastered. It would plot their position on the curriculum rather than record their performance on only one level of it.

An important function of assessment is often omitted when assessment is used for grading. This is the function of providing helpful immediate feedback. When testing for grades, an error is no more than a red mark on a paper to be tallied. We must keep in mind that correct answers are learned only by getting the correct answer enough times to commit it to memory. Errors indicate that this is not going on, and in some learning activities it indicates that incorrect answers are being learned.

Errors indicate that learning is not occurring or, if it is, it is of the wrong kind. This is important information and should not simply be left as a red mark and imbedded in the score total at the top of a paper. Errors should be identified as quickly as possible. Then the student should be provided with the correct response. Errors should not be left uncorrected.

The errors students make may indicate more than just a single wrong answer. The error may be part of a larger pattern of errors already learned. Errors may indicate that a readiness stage has not been reached and that necessary prerequisites are missing. Attention to errors with the purpose of giving helpful corrective feedback is a fundamental purpose of assessment, and it is another way that assessment should be integrated with instruction. Grading separates assessment from these important instructional functions.

When teachers prepare tests in order to give grades, they are often not concerned with how closely the test items relate to what has actually been taught. Teachers may be concerned with making items that are sufficiently discriminating so that not every student will get them right. It doesn't really matter that the test does not precisely reflect the content of what was taught if its sole purpose is to give grades. No substantive feedback comes from such tests and the results will not be, nor could they be, used to make curricular adjustments for individual students. When students take such tests, they may look at each other in bewilderment, wondering where the teacher got these test items. Grades have greatly distorted assessment, making it totally separate from instruction. Once again, assessment should be integrated with instruction insuring the match between student and curriculum.

Chapter 12

CURRICULUM–BASED ASSESSMENT

Curriculum-based assessment (CBA) is emerging as an alternative to traditional forms of educational testing. This is the form of assessment that I advocate. Many of the central principles of CBA have been discussed at various points throughout the book. However, since CBA and conventional grading systems are often in direct conflict, a closer look at the system is needed.

There is another reason for a closer look at CBA. As it has emerged over the past few years, it has taken on somewhat different interpretations and different forms. The form of CBA that I advocate is fundamentally defined by Tucker (1987, 1985), Gickling and Thompson (1985), and Hargis (1987, 1982).

The characteristic that unites the various forms of CBA is the belief that assessment should be taken from the curriculum in use. The principle differences between the form of CBA that I prefer and the others concern two things. The first of these is that success be the guiding principle underlying assessment. The second difference is that ongoing instructional activity itself should be the basis for most of the assessment activity. Assessment should be part and parcel of instruction. A student's performance on the work actually being done on a daily basis should be observed and analyzed. Assessment should not be a separate and even an intrusive activity.

When I use the term CBA, it is this specific form, delineated above, to which I refer.

CBA is an intimate, integral part of instruction. Normal assessment procedures are isolated from teaching; CBA incorporates them. The curriculum itself becomes the basic form for assessment. The activities that make up daily instructional processes become tests. Assessment is thus made constant and direct. Assessment in CBA is not separate from instruction; it is a main part of instructional activity.

Using an instructional activity for assessment is like using the activity as an inventory. The activities themselves become informal inventories.

79

Whether reading or math, introduction or drill for mastery, the performance of students is constantly monitored. The number right and wrong are checked, and the level of comprehension is measured on reading and activities that require reading. However, rather than simply marking, tallying, and scoring in order to give a grade, the data is used to see if the difficulty level of the activity is matched to the student and the student is experiencing success. The number of incorrect items is checked to see if too many unfamiliar items have been used in the activity.

CBA makes instruction a dynamic, fluid process. Teaching and testing do not move in rigid lock-step increments, compelling all students to move in unison. Since the curriculum and the routine instruction that presents it daily are used as the primary tests, the curriculum and instructional activity must change to fit individual students. It must change to an appropriate level of difficulty so that instructional-level scores are always being produced. This constant testing and adjusting keeps the process dynamic. Static systems produce a distribution of grades and a substantial percentage of failure. Testing in the conventional educational setting is only a reflection of how individual students are doing within a lock-step curriculum or compared to others in his or her age group in the lock-step system.

Assessment for grading usually treats errors as mere marks, something to tally. In CBA, the type of error should be examined as well. Errors are used in providing helpful corrective feedback. Errors are not treated as just a mark, and if they are not, students will be much less likely to be practicing them.

Errors are an important consideration in CBA, but the emphasis is more on what has been done correctly and mastered. Success is a central concern of CBA, so the selection and preparation of instructional activities and materials that are doable is the function of assessment information. Doable activities are made up of material that is familiar, mastered or on its way to being so. This provides helpful supporting context for newly introduced items. It permits successful review and drill for items on their way to mastery. Finding out what a student knows or has mastered is a major concern of CBA, especially when trying to find where to start with students. This is almost the opposite of most conventional diagnostic testing. In conventional systems of diagnostic testing, one is specifically looking for deficiencies in skills or subskills. The focus is on deficiencies. The remedial activities prescribed as a result of this kind of diagnostic testing will be entirely devoted to the missing or defective subskills. Since the emphasis is on weakness, the remedial activities are often frustratingly difficult and the results are often disappointing.

Success is the essential focus of CBA, so only the number of new items or skills can be introduced and practiced that students can do correctly. Many instructional activities require reading and so must be made up mostly of known words and content matter. Remember, by definition, the instructional reading level must be made up of over 95 percent known words. With some students, it takes a great effort to find enough known words to prepare reading materials. Unknown words and missing skills are easy to find, but activities that are largely made up of them are frustratingly difficult and do not produce good results. Success must be planned and structured into learning activities. Structuring success requires careful attention to what a student can do.

Typical diagnostic tests do not represent any particular curriculum. However, with CBA, assessment must be representitive of the curriculum. CBA addresses the problem of test validity in a straightforward way. It insures test validity by making certain that the content of the test is made up of what is being taught.

We simply assume the validity of most diagnostic tests. However, they may have little content validity. They are not likely to accurately measure what has been taught on a particular curriculum. To the extent they do not measure what has been taught, they lack content validity. The problem caused by having respected, but content invalid, diagnostic tests is that they become an additional curriculum. These tests invariably reveal skill deficits in the referred students. It should be obvious that if the tests don't sample skills being taught from the curriculum being used, they will show deficiencies. If items being assessed are not taught, certainly they are more likely to be missed. The importance of such skill deficiencies is actually negligible. Their mistaken importance is gained from the simple fact that they appeared on a test which is imagined to have validity. Since the test is mistakenly viewed as valid, the skill deficits measured by them are viewed as significant impediments to learning. As a consequence, these skills are taught; they have become another curriculum. This new curriculum, which is made up of questionable content, will displace time normally devoted to regular curricular work.

CBA requires that tests be samples of the curriculum in use. The best way to assure that tests have content validity is to make them up from curricular items. Selecting tests is a potentially risky business. Choose them well, for they may become your curriculum. If we assume a test is valid, we are virtually compelled to teach to what the results dictate.

This notion leads to another important dictum of CBA. It is appropriate to teach to tests. In fact, CBA is the ultimate in teaching the test. After all, if a test is worth giving, it is worth teaching to. Why give a test if you are not going to act on its results. Test what you teach and teach what you test. This is how content validity is attained and how real progress is measured.

Grades and CBA do not mix. When assessment procedures are used to identify the instructional levels of students with the objective of making each student succeed, it is not possible to give a distribution of grades. The levels of performance should indicate the instructional level is being maintained for all students. Everyone should be achieving these performance levels. The instructional levels in any classroom will necessarily cover a range of difficulty. This level must be matched to each student. In other words, the difficulty of the work must be at various levels in order to keep the scores in the same range for all students. This is the opposite of what happens when assessment is used for giving grades.

Classrooms where students receive a wide distribution of grades are classrooms where no real attention is given to individual differences in academic ability. CBA focuses assessment attention on individual differences. When CBA is implemented, no such distributions of grades are possible.

CBA compels teachers to use alternative systems of reporting progress. These systems are of necessity substantive, not normative. Substantive reports are precise statements of where and on what students are working. They are much more useful than grades or scores. This information can be used to plot progress and to find readiness and entry levels.

CBA provides the principle procedure for the identification of learning disabilities. Many lower-achieving students acquire the learning disabled label as a discrepancy emerges between their potential for achievement and their actual achievement. CBA requires that to be considered learning disabled, students' learning problems persist after the best match between instructional level and instructional difficulty has been made. If there is a residual problem, then there may well be a real learning disability. First, in every case, the curriculum mismatch must be ruled out as the cause.

Unfortunately, failure is our primary diagnostic tool. Using failure in this way leads to other assessment practices that are fruitless and resource draining. When students fail, we seek a cause in the student, not in the curriculum. We look for a variety of student deficiencies. We may look for a deficiency in some theoretical aptitude, either cognitive or perceptual. Attention deficit disorders are currently a popular problem to look for. Many tests have been created to find these various deficits. Students who are failing will be given these tests, and the areas on them with the lower scores will invariably be considered as deficiencies in essential skills and therefore the cause of the students' learning problems. Remedial treatments designed to overcome the deficits or to bypass the deficit area will be prepared. These treatments constitute new curricula for the students. Results of such treatment programs are almost always disappointing or equivocal. The real problem, the curricular mismatch, has been overlooked. This is a principle of CBA: The curriculum must first be ruled out as a cause of learning disabilities. The residual problems that persist after this is done can then be used as evidence of a learning problem which may need to be the focus of special curricular intervention.

Finding the cause of a learning problem is important. There are causes outside the curriculum and within students. However, failure because of a mismatch with the curriculum is the most common cause of learning problems, and it is unfortunately overlooked most of the time.

Chapter 13

ALTERNATIVES TO GRADES

Grading has become the end-all and be-all of most testing. I have argued that grades are a poor product to get from such a large effort. Expecting such a product distorts the form and purposes of a potentially useful activity. The result of assessment should be information that is useful for instruction. The result should give substantive information on what students have learned. When assessment effort goes to producing grades, the activity is separated from instruction; it is even separated from learning.

We do need to report student progress, but we must do this with something that does not have so many negative and often damaging consequences. We need a simple procedure for this reporting. Grades may have a single virtue. This is their simplicity. They are easily and quickly recorded by teachers, and they are readily understood by parents.

Grades are basically normative. They either show how students are doing compared to other students in their classroom or they show how the students are performing on the curricular material assigned to fit the norm for a particular grade or class. We need substantive rather than normative methods of reporting progress. We need a simple report of what individuals are learning and what they have mastered. We need a system of reporting that assures that all students are getting instruction at the curricular levels appropriate to each of them and not one that compels diverse groups of students to work at only one level.

The alternative should make all parties concerned, teachers, students, and parents, learning oriented rather than grade oriented. Students should not be engaged in instructional activities just to get a grade. They should be engaged in order to learn. This will require a major reordering of our attitudes.

We have institutionalized the lock-step curricular organization of our schools and the grading system that perpetuates it. We need to change our orientation to one which requires continuous progress for every student, and we must accept the fact that students learn at remarkably varied rates. We need a reporting system that fosters continuous progress. We will have to learn to use substantive information and rely less on normative figures.

If continuous progress for every student is the goal, an appropriate starting level, or entry point on the curriculum, must be ascertained on each student. This will be the highest level where each student can work successfully. After the entry level has been determined, daily instructional activities that lead to progress along the curricular ladder must be closely monitored to make sure that the instructional-level match is being maintained. At the end of the learning period a final assessment is made of the items that were taught. The results of this assessment constitutes the final report. It should show progress along the curricular ladder. The amount of progress can be plotted much the same as with a growth chart.

For some time, this form of assessment has been recommended (NEA, 1974). Criterion-referenced testing (testing that seeks to determine how well students have mastered specific learning objectives) lends itself to this quite well. Identifying the point of entry has been called formative assessment, and the measurement of mastery at various points along the way has been called summative assessment. Curriculum-based assessment has advanced these ideas, including the routine instructional activities as a major part of assessment and the focus on the need for success. With curriculum-based assessment we have available the information necessary to make substantive progress reports at all stages of the instructional process.

The most useful reports of a student's attainments are the inventories or tests themselves. The major summative tests can be abstracted to curricular checklists that simply indicate what specific curricular items each student has mastered. These kinds of reports are helpful to teachers as students move from grade level to grade level or transfer between schools. In this latter instance, the inventories will allow the new teachers to compare the new students' curricular background to that of the curriculum they are entering. Grades in general subject areas cannot reflect the varying content that makes up the subjects in different schools.

How much detail in these reports do parents want or how much can they tolerate? Parents obviously will be enormously varied in their interest in, and ability to understand, substantive progress reports. A simple summary such as a graph or chart may suffice, but the entire summative report of progress along the curriculum should be available.

The daily work the students are engaged in should be taken home for the parents to review. The work itself should be viewed as the primary progress report. It shows the specific work and level where each student is.

This will not provide the normative information that some parents will want. They will want to know where their child's work is in relation to others in his or her group. This information is easy enough to supply. A simple statement of what the average students are doing and where their child is relative to that position should be enough.

It is even possible to extrapolate a letter grade from this information if parents demand it. The instructional levels of students will form a distribution just as grades do in a lock-step setting. The students with the lowest instructional levels would be getting the lowest grades in those lock-step situations, and so these students could be given a low letter grade to show this possible position. The same is true for the students with the higher instructional levels, except they would be assigned the high grades. It would have to be noted that these grades are only hypothetical for the lower-achieving students, however, since none of the students would actually be permitted to fail or do failing work.

Using substantive progress reports keeps teachers' attention focused on assessment for instructional purposes. Measurement activities should be for determining the specifics of what individuals are learning. Attention to these details is the important feature of individualized instruction, curriculum-based assessment, and continuous progress models of instruction. Grading alters the focus of assessment from instruction and works against the implementation of these effective instructional procedures.

The individual educational plan (IEP) required by Public Law 94–142 for use with handicapped students provides an alternative for grades. Assessment is used to find the student's current state of functioning, from which point both short-term and long-term objectives are formulated. Progress toward the attainment of these objectives are measured, and the plan itself is periodically reformulated. Progress reports are substantive and are based upon the IEP objectives.

Reports can be checklists indicating those objectives mastered and those being learned. Reports can be narrative descriptions of what has been learned and what is in progress. Self-reports are useful without the pressure of grades. Writing about work in progress is a helpful learning activity, and self-diagnosis of problems is a useful way of clarifying and identifying problems. Again, this is more helpful if there is no threat of grades. Revealing apparent weaknesses will not be an issue. The work the students do daily should be used as the report of ongoing activity leading to the various curricular objectives.

The use of routine work in the assessment and reporting of progress compliments its use in providing helpful feedback to students. Grades provide no helpful feedback. In the process of checking routine work, the students can be given quick corrective feedback which aids in learning and prevents error practice. This assessment provides feedback to the teacher as well, and it gives direction in how to adjust the activity to produce success and progress.

The work being taken home as a report should reflect two things. It should show the parents the items and the level of work being done on the curriculum, and it should show that the work is being done successfully. There should be no papers being brought home covered with red marks and poor grades. This is evidence that the teacher is not meeting the instructional needs of that student. Progress can be plotted by contrasting the work being done over time.

If grades must be used, do we need F's? Recently, a minor flap occurred in the news when it was revealed that Stanford University as a matter of policy did not have the F among its letter grades. This has been a policy since the 1960s. Had F's been missed? Apparently not. When institutions are very selective in their admissions policies, it makes no sense to artificially place some of these academically able students at risk for a failing grade simply because there is a failing grade. A substantial number of prestigious, highly selective professional schools use no grades at all. This does not mean that there are not means for evaluating and rating students. The evaluation must now focus on substantive characteristics and accomplishments of the students.

In the case of the public schools, the admissions policies are necessarily quite open. However, the learning opportunities are not open to all. Failing grades are the evidence that some students are excluded. Of course, simply doing away with the grade will not assure that the students will be able to learn. That opportunity occurs only when teachers match the instructional level to student ability. Still, having a failing grade remains a barrier to doing that, and the existence of grades means that there is a policy of permitting some students to be excluded from learning.

Eliminating grades might encourage teachers to try to give even the lowest-achieving students work which they can do passably well.

Chapter 14

INSTRUCTION WITHOUT GRADES:
NONCOMPETITIVE AND COOPERATIVE LEARNING

Grades create competitive, noncooperative learning environments. Cheating routinely occurs and is a behavior readily learned and accepted in such environments. Competition for grades changes the focus from learning to getting a grade. The normal social nature of learning that goes on outside of school is replaced by isolated artificial activities. Schools are not socially healthy, supportive places in which to learn.

Without grades, noncompetitive and cooperative learning environments that focus on learning can be used. Success and cooperation can be emphasized. All students are to do well and get things correct. Everyone is encouraged to help each other. Cheating is irrelevant. Some noncompetitive systems include supervised study, peer tutoring, and cooperative learning teams. A different model of teaching is also possible, one that is student centered rather than teacher centered. This is a model of teaching designed to avoid the problems described in the chapter on the specialist system.

Many elements of teaching without grades have been discussed in previous parts of the book. Curriculum-based assessment is one. It requires that success and continuous progress for each student be dominating features. The actual delivery of instruction in such classrooms requires a very different model of teaching.

The classroom must be well organized to keep the students engaged at a variety of individual instructional levels. It is theoretically possible to have each individual student working independently with teacher supervision and monitoring. However, this would take enormous care in the selection and preparation of instructional materials. To alleviate this, cooperative grouping arrangements can be used. There is ample evidence that cooperative learning and peer tutoring are effective and improve achievement of the students involved. To make these systems work requires planning, organizational, and management skills. Much of the teacher's time is devoted to supervising, observing, and measuring, as well as to materials preparation and selection.

Student time on task increases, and, as a consequence, the amount of material consumed increases much more rapidly than in the traditional teacher-centered room. Topping (1988) stated that the rate of progress and consumption in cooperative learning programs can prove an embarrassment when it is found that the stock of available and relevant materials is exhausted.

Individually arranged, supervised study is helpful, and even necessary, when a teacher has a student who has a distinct interest or ability level. It is a good technique to use when teachers find a highly academically talented student in their rooms. It is also necessary when they find a student with a readiness deficit that places them too far outside one or more of the cooperative learning teams.

Peer tutoring can be arranged in a number of ways. When classrooms are organized cooperatively, students learn to help each other. As a student finishes an activity, he or she will be expected to assist the next student through the same process. Students are expected to help each other on anything they can. There are many opportunities for this kind of informal peer assistance in noncompetitive classroom arrangements. There are currently in use several organized peer tutoring arrangements. They include pairing students of similar ability, different abilities, and different age levels.

In general, when we speak of cooperative learning today, it means placing students in four- to five-member groups of mixed ability. After initial instruction by the teacher, the students work together cooperatively on worksheets or other practice materials until each student in the group gets the correct answers. The students discuss the answers, reach consensus, drill each other, and assess one another to make certain that each group member will demonstrate mastery when assessed individually by the teacher. The students' scores on these individual assessments can be summed to form group or team scores. These scores are used to provide recognition to the team.

The success of the team requires cooperation. There is an incentive for all students to do well and for all students to help their teammates. As students provide one another with explanations of concepts or skills, they themselves gain in achievement. This cycle of cooperative learning significantly increases student achievement.

Cooperative, rather than competitive, orientations are very important for the low-achieving and disadvantaged members of any classroom. These children, almost by definition, are unable to compete for grades in regular classroom organizations. Competition for them means coming in last and getting failing grades. In cooperative learning arrangements, all students must perform well. It is the role of each student to assist each of the other students in learning and performing well. No one is to fail. Additionally, in the act of assisting each other, learning is further enhanced in the helpers.

When teachers and students expect everyone to do well and everyone cooperates with each other to this end, chronic failure experiences stop. When this happens, the students' self-esteem and confidence can reach normal levels. When all students are expected and assisted to do well, they can feel accepted and secure.

Instruction becomes much more student centered in cooperative learning arrangements. When instruction is teacher centered, students waste much of the day. Thurlow et al. (1984) found that the average second grade student reads aloud about 90 seconds per day as they take their turn to read in the 10- to 25-member reading groups. While the teacher is working with one reading group, the other students are working with activities that take little supervision. These are the "follow-up" activities which make up the major part of the school day and are of questionable quality. Further, the time on task during follow-up activities is quite low (Stevens et al., 1987).

With cooperative learning arrangements, teacher-centered instruction is reduced and student-engaged time is increased. Achievement is directly related to engaged time. Students in two- to five-member learning teams can be engaged and assisted much more extensively than they can in the ten- to twenty-five-member teacher-centered groups. The quality of engaged time is greatly enhanced. The students get constant immediate feedback. Little opportunity exists to practice errors. Everyone is to get everything correct. Further, the students that are assisting also benefit from time engaged in the activities.

Students that fail in competitive grade-oriented classrooms need cooperative approaches. Competition is only motivating for those students with sufficient skill and ability to be competitive. Grades motivate only students who can get good grades. In competitive classrooms, when students realize there is little hope for doing well, there is a strong temptation to cheat. There is no temptation to cheat when everyone is to do well as a matter of policy. Another benefit is the elimination of the problem behaviors resulting from the inability to be competitive and the frustration of chronic failure.

Cooperative learning can make at-risk students effective learners. It must be remembered, though, that not all learners operate at the same level of efficiency. If the curriculum is assigned to grade levels in lock step, even cooperative learning arrangements may have limited benefit. All students must be permitted to work at their individual instructional levels, not grade levels. They should be placed on an individual path of continuous progress, not a lock-step path that produces casualties.

Cooperative activity need not be restricted to the students. Teachers can act cooperatively. There is actually a great deal of overlap in the achievement levels of students from one grade to the next. Teachers can react against the sharply drawn boundaries between grades. They need not feel an isolated duty to their place on the curriculum. The barriers that isolate grades should be broken down by cooperative effort among teachers. Teachers should plan for cooperative learning activities for students with overlapping abilities between grade levels. This would permit continuous progress for students working at many different levels. When teachers develop such cooperative arrangements many of the negative effects of the lock-step curriculum are mitigated.

In an earlier chapter I discussed the problem of the specialist teacher. Specialization has caused more isolation and has reduced the opportunity for cooperative effort. At the elementary level it is specialization by grade, and at the secondary level it is specialization by subject area.

Specialization contributes to the most destructive problems of the lock step at the secondary level. Hordes of students move through the specialists' rooms each day. Some may see 150 or more different students. With so many different students, the entire individual attention each student may get will be devoted to grading. Teachers will have little opportunity to do more than score papers in order to give grades.

Teachers should not have to deal with so many different students. Teachers should teach more subject areas to fewer students over longer time periods. They then can become more familiar with individual student performance and their instructional needs. Cooperative learning arrangements are possible. The teachers can devote much more time to the production of materials and planning, time that would normally be devoted to scoring for grades. Cooperative teamwork activities will engage the students for much of each day.

When teachers enter cooperative arrangements with other teachers, they can gain still more time for planning and the production of materials. Cooperation among teachers can increase the array of materials available. Multilevels of materials will be necessary to match the many ability levels of students. If teachers over two or more grade levels cooperate, the levels of materials available will naturally increase as the resources are combined.

With the wider range of materials and the overlapping range of abilities in combined classes, cooperative teams can incorporate different ability levels more effectively. Transition problems between grades are eased, and teachers can stay in contact with students for two or more years.

In traditional competitive classrooms, Rasinski (1988) points out that teachers isolate students communicatively and physically. They are constantly told to work alone, work quietly, and stop talking. The students are isolated from social interaction and placed in intensive competition with each other. Students are urged to be "number one," to be a "winner." Scores and accumulated points are graphically displayed to show the relative standings of each member of the class. Rasinski feels that it is difficult for students to learn citizenship and cooperation when the teacher turns the classroom community into a classroom of isolated individuals. Each individual is learning to seek her or his own personal gain at the expense of others. In these competitive, graded environments, students are lead to believe that cooperation and helping others are not important parts of the classroom or the community outside.

REFERENCES

Ashlock, R. B. (1986). *Error patterns in computation* (4th ed.). Columbus: Merrill.

Bellanca, J. A. (1977). *Grading.* Washington: NEA.

Cremin, L. A. (1961). *The transformation of the school: Progressivism in American education 1876-1957.* New York: Knopf.

Cureton, W. L. (1971). The history of grading practices. *NCME, 2,* 1–8.

Evans, F. B. (1976). What research says about grading. In S. B. Simon and J. A. Bellanca (Eds.), *Degrading the grading myths: A primer of alternatives to grades and marks* (pp. 30–50). Washington: Association for Supervision and Curriculum Development.

Gickling, E. E., and Thompson, V. (1985). A personal view of curriculum-based assessment. *Exceptional Children, 52,* 205–218.

Glasser, W. (1971). *The effect of school failure on the life of a child.* Washington: National Association of Elementary School Principals.

Glasser, W. (1986). *Control Theory in the Classroom.* New York: Harper and Row.

Grimes, L. (1981). Learned helplessness and attribution theory: Redefining children's learning problems. *Learning Disability Quarterly, 4,* 91–100.

Haney, W. (1984). Testing reasoning and reasoning about testing. *Review of Educational Research, 54,* 597–654.

Hargis, C. H. (1987). *Curriculum based assessment: A primer.* Springfield: Charles C Thomas.

Hargis, C. H. (1989). *Teaching low achieving and disadvantaged students.* Springfield: Charles C Thomas.

Hargis, C. H. (1982). *Teaching reading to handicapped children.* Denver: Love.

Hargis, C. H., Terhaar-Yonkers, M., Williams, P. C., and Reed, M. T. (1988). Repetition requirements for word recognition. *Journal of Reading, 31,* 320–327.

Hargis, C. H., and Terhaar-Yonkers, M. (1989). Do grades cause learning disabilities? *Holistic Education Review, 2,* 14–18.

Kronick, R., and Hargis, C. H. (1990). *Dropouts: Who drops out and why...and the recommended action.* Springfield: Charles C Thomas.

Kirschenbaum, H., Napier, R., and Simon, S. B. (1971). *Wad-ja-get? The grading game in American education.* New York: Hart Publishing Co.

Marshall, M. S. (1968). *Teaching without grades.* Corvallis: Oregon State University Press.

Milton, O., Pollio, H. R., and Eison, J. A. (1986). *Making sense of college grades.* San Francisco: Jossey-Bass.

NEA. (1974). *Evaluation and reporting of student achievement.* Washington: Author.

Nicolson, F. W. (1917). Standardizing the marking system. *Educational Review, 54,* 225–237.

Rasinski, T. V. (1988). Caring and cooperation in the reading curriculum. *The Reading Teacher, 41,* 632–634.

Rosenshine, B. V., and Berliner, D. C. (1978). Academic engaged time. *British Journal of Teacher Education, 4,* 3–16.

Shriner, J., and Salvia, J. (1988). Chronic noncorrespondence between elementary math curricula and arithmetic tests. *Exceptional Children, 55,* 240–248.

Simon, S. B., and Bellanca, J. A. (Eds.). (1976). *Degrading the grading myths: A primer of alternatives to grades and marks.* Washington: Association for Supervision and Curriculum Development.

Slavin, R. E. (1989). On mastery learning and mastery teaching. *Educational Leadership, 46,* 77–79.

Slavin, R. E., and Madden, N. A. (1989). What works for students at risk: A research synthesis. *Educational Leadership, 46,* 4–13.

Smith, A., and Dobbin, J. E. (1960). Marks and marking systems. In C. W. Harris (Ed.): *The encyclopedia of educational research* (pp. 783–791). New York: Macmillan.

Stanovich, K. E. (1986). Matthew effects in reading: Some consequences of individual differences in the acquisition of literacy. *Reading Research Quarterly, 21,* 360–407.

Starch, D., and Elliott, E. C. (1912). Reliability of grading high school work in English. *School Review,* 1912, *20,* 442–457.

Starch, D., and Elliott, E. C. (1913). Reliability of grading work in mathematics. *School Review, 21,* 254–259.

Stevens, R. J., Madden, N. A., Slavin, R. E., and Farnish, A. M. (1987). Cooperative integrated reading and composition: Two field experiments. *Reading Research Quarterly, 22,* 433–454.

Stone, B., Cundick, B. P., and Swanson, D. (1988). Special education screening system: Group achievement test. *Exceptional Children, 55,* 71–75.

Thompson, V. P., Gickling, E. E., and Havertape, J. F. (1983). The effects of medication and curriculum on task-related behaviors of attention deficit disordered and low achieving peers. *Monographs in behavioral disorders: Severe behavior disorders of children and youth.* CCBD, Arizona State University. Series #6.

Thurlow, M., Groden, J., Ysseldyke, J., and Algozzine, R. (1984). Student reading during reading class: The lost activity in reading instruction. *Journal of Educational Research, 77,* 267–272.

Topping, K. (1988). *The peer tutoring handbook: Promoting cooperative learning.* Beckenham, Kent: Croom Helm Ltd.

Tucker, J. A. (1985). Curriculum-based assessment: An introduction. *Exceptional Children, 52,* 199–204.

Tucker, J. A. (1987, Fall). Curriculum-based assessment is no fad. *The Collaborative Educator,* pp. 4, 10.

Wrinkle, W. L. (1947). *Improving marking and reporting practices in elementary and secondary schools.* New York: Holt, Rinehart and Winston.

INDEX